Little Bo-Peep

A pantomime

Paul Reakes

Samuel French — London
www.samuelfrench-london.co.uk

FOR AMATEUR PRODUCTION ENQUIRIES

UNITED KINGDOM AND WORLD
EXCLUDING NORTH AMERICA
plays@samuelfrench.co.uk
020 7255 4302/01

Each title is subject to availability from Samuel French,
depending upon country of performance.

CHARACTERS

Fanny Fairacre, of Fairacre farm
Wally, her pig boy
Freddie Fairacre, her son
Lady Sneering, a scheming aristocrat
Little Bo-Peep, a shepherdess
Ding ⎫
Dong ⎭ part of Cindy's troupe
Cindy Sparkle, of Sparkle's Sparkling Spectacular
Mefisto, an evil magician
Buttercup, the cow
PC Wurld, of the local constabulary
Merdalf, another magician

Chorus of: **Villagers, Sheep, Show Dancers,
Barmaids, Farmhands** and **Dwellers** of the Place of
the Disappeared

SYNOPSIS OF SCENES

ACT I
SCENE 1   The Village Green
SCENE 2   Near the Farm
SCENE 3   In the Show Tent
SCENE 4   Near the Farm
SCENE 5   The Village Green, that night

ACT II
SCENE 1   Fanny's Farmyard
SCENE 2   Near the Farm
SCENE 3   In the Show Tent
SCENE 4   Near the Farm
SCENE 5   The Place of the Disappeared
SCENE 6   Near the Farm
SCENE 7   The Grand Finale

Time — Pantotime

MUSICAL NUMBERS

ACT I

No 1	Song and Dance	Villagers
No 2	Comedy Song	Fanny, Freddie and Wally
No 3	Romantic Song	Freddie and Villagers
No 4	Song and Dance	Bo-Peep, Freddie and Sheep
No 5	Romantic Duet and Dance	Freddie and Bo-Peep
No 6	Song and Dance	Cindy, Ding and Dong
No 7	Song and Dance	Cindy and Show Dancers
No 7a	Reprise of Song 5 (optional)	Freddie and Bo-Peep
No 8	Song and Dance	Villagers and Barmaids
No 9	Lullaby	Bo-Peep and Sheep

ACT II

No 10	Song and Dance	Farmhands
No 11	Song and Dance	Fanny, Freddie, Bo-Peep, Wally and Farmhands
No 12	Comedy Song	Ding and Dong
No 13	Song and Dance	Cindy and Show Dancers
No 14	Comedy "Romantic" Song	Wally and Cindy
No 15	Romantic Duet	Freddie and Bo-Peep
No 16	Dance	Dwellers
No 17	Song	All
No 18	House Song	Fanny, Wally, Ding, Dong and Audience
No 19	Finale Song or Reprise	All

CHARACTERS AND COSTUMES

Fanny Fairacre (Dame) owns and runs the farm. She is a buxom, rumbustious "lady", who is always on friendly and confidential terms with the audience. She never misses an opportunity of letting them know her opinions on the proceedings and the other characters. Although she is prone to sarcasm, she must be a likeable old girl. It goes without saying that all her costumes, hair-dos and make-up should be outrageous and funny. Comically suitable for a female farmer. Special Finale costume.

Wally (Comedian) is a lovable local yokel. He is not too bright, and his gormless expression, shambling appearance and "Mummerset" accent doesn't help. He also has to display his romantic yearnings for Cindy Sparkle. This should be played mainly for laughs, but with a touch of pathos. Good comic characterization and camaraderie with the audience is essential. Shabby rustic smock, battered hat and turned down wellies. When he pays court to Cindy, he wears a loud check suit that is far too small, and a hat that is far too big. A gaudy tie and a huge flower in his buttonhole complete his ensemble.

Freddie (Principal Boy) helps his mum to run the farm. He is a very handsome young fellow with tremendous charm, a winning smile and lovely manners. He also has the best pair of legs to be found in agricultural circles! These virtues certainly appeal to Lady Sneering! Needless to say, he is deeply in love with Little Bo-Peep, and will do anything to protect her. A strong singing voice and dancing ability is required. His costumes, although rustic, should be smart and attractive. Special Finale costume.

Lady Sneering (Baddie) is an obnoxious aristocrat. She is haughty, arrogant, spoilt, scheming, jealous ... the list goes on! Her contempt for all "commoners" should guarantee plenty of unfavourable responses from the audience. Determined to have Freddie all to herself, she enlists the services of Mefisto, the magician, to remove the competition, Little Bo-Peep. Possessing lots of money, and a very skilled beautician, her age is indeterminate. We might put a guess at somewhere between 35 and 45. A strong, dominant personality is essential. All her costumes and accessories are richly ostentatious.

Little Bo-Peep (Principal Girl) is a young shepherdess. She is pretty, petite and very charming. She is never soppy or simpering. Who could blame Freddie for being head over heels in love with her? She is rather naive though, never suspecting that Lady Sneering has designs on her boyfriend. She is very good at looking after the sheep, until she falls asleep and allows her woolly charges to be spirited away! A pleasant singing voice and dancing ability is required. Delightful "Dresden" shepherdess-style costumes, complete with shepherd's crook. Special Finale costume.

Ding and **Dong** (Comedy Duo) As performers in Cindy Sparkle's show they are pretty inept, but they make up for it by being a likeable pair of nitwits. Ding appears to be the more intelligent. They are very fond of Cindy and the feeling is mutual. In fact, it would be hard to imagine anyone else giving them employment. Good comic timing and camaraderie with the audience is essential. They are written to played as a male duo, but this can be changed, with the necessary alterations in the script, to a male/female or an all female partnership. Their costumes are theatrically flamboyant but showing signs of wear and tear.

Cindy Sparkle is the attractive and shapely young woman who owns the travelling show. To the public she is full of razzmatazz and showbiz vitality. In private she is subdued and beset by business problems. When Wally declares his love for her, it comes as a surprise that someone like Cindy reciprocates. But that's love, and the topsy-turvy world of Pantomime! Singing and dancing ability is a must for this role as this is what Cindy specializes in. Her show costumes are flamboyant and glitzy, showing plenty of leg in spangled tights. She also gets to wear a Clown costume and mask.

Mefisto, the magician (Baddie) is the main attraction of Cindy's show. Using this, he threatens to leave unless she pays him more money. Apart from being skilled at conventional stage magic, (see Production Notes) he has command of other powers which are far more dark and sinister. Although an instrument of the scheming Lady Sneering, he is defiantly a "Baddie" in his own right and should receive his fair share of boos and hisses. An egotistical personality is essential. He wears bizarre robes and headgear, decorated with strange magical symbols. A pair of curling eyebrows and a forked beard will add to his sinister appearance.

Buttercup is a friendly cow who has swallowed two people! She also has the facility to produce a bottle of milk, butter and a box of chocolates! The milking routine should be carefully thought out and well rehearsed.

A good cow skin with movable mouth and eyelashes. A natty straw hat decorated with flowers for the Finale.

PC Wurld is the village bobby, from the good old days when every village had one. He is slow and plodding, but very conscious of his "dooty". Called in to investigate some missing sheep, he is utterly bewildered by the strange events which follow. After all, it's not every day you're made to disappear while walking the beat! He eventually comes into his own when he arrests nasty Lady Sneering. Old-fashioned Police Constable's uniform with helmet, belt and big boots.

Merdalf is another magician. Fortunately, he is one of the good and friendly variety. He wastes no time in using his superior powers to dispense with Mefisto, and bring about a happy ending for all concerned. This role requires a commanding presence with the ability to show kindness and humour. He can be Merlin/Gandalf-like in appearance, with flowing white hair and beard, but this is not compulsory. Over his ragged robe he wears the same hooded cloak as the other Dwellers. Resplendent robe and tall magician's hat for the Finale.

There are several small speaking parts for the Villagers and Farmhands. There is also a Publican, which can be male or female.

The Chorus appear as Villagers, Farmhands and Dwellers of The Place of the Disappeared. For the latter, their rustic costumes are concealed under hooded cloaks that give them a sinister and menacing appearance. The cloaks can be easily removed after they exit during the black-out to reappear as Villagers/Farmhands towards the end of the scene.

The Dancers appear as Villagers, Show Dancers, Barmaids, Farmhands and Dwellers of The Place of the Disappeared. Picturesque rustic costumes for the Villagers/Farmhands. Their show costumes are glitzy and exotic. They also require Clown costumes and masks. For the Barmaids, they wear rustic skirts and blouses with white mob caps and aprons. As the Dwellers they wear an abbreviated version of the hooded cloaks worn by the Chorus. If desired, they need only participate in the opening dance sequence of this scene.

The Children appear as Village Children and Little Bo-Peep's sheep. It is advisable to have two separate groups. The actual size of your "flock" is left to the individual director/choreographer, but it would be advisable not to make it too large. Perhaps six or eight? It must be remembered that they are required to exit very quickly during a complete black-out, and are involved in a chase sequence in Act II, Scene 5. Costumes for the Village Children should be picturesque rustic. I will not even suggest how you turn your little darlings into sheep! I am sure your ingenious costume designers, wardrobe and make-up departments will have their own ideas, and will work wonders.

PRODUCTION NOTES

STAGING

The pantomime offers opportunities for elaborate staging, but can be produced quite simply if funds and facilities are limited.

There are four full sets :
> The Village Green
> In the Show Tent
> Fanny's Farmyard
> The Place of the Disappeared

These scenes are interlinked by one front cloth:
> Near the farm

There can be a special Finale setting, or the Village Green set can be used with added decorations.

The Village Green
Pantomime representation of an idyllic country village. Quaint cottages and shops, an old inn, shady trees, and a view of the countryside with Fanny's farm in the distance.

Near the Farm
This is a front cloth used to interlink all the full stage settings. It is painted to represent a picturesque country road. If this is not practical, Tabs can be used.

In the Show Tent
The back cloth and side wings represent the tent's stripped interior with entrances on both sides. Across the back, on a raised platform, are rows of brightly painted benches for the spectators. There are smaller single benches downstage on both sides. Like a circus ring, the artists perform "in the round". On the surface it is colourful and glitzy, but as this is a travelling show there are distinct signs of wear and tear.

Fanny's Farmyard

Another depiction of idyllic rural bliss. A picturesque thatched farmhouse, an old wooden barn (both with practical doors), a low fence, and a view of the countryside with the village in the distance.

The Place of the Disappeared

This is where Mefisto's victims find themselves after he has made them disappear. It is a nightmarish and surreal world that even Salvador Dali would find disconcerting! Unearthly, uncanny, and above all, very unpleasant. How you create this loathsome limbo land is left to the fertile imaginations of your director and set designer. It could be achieved by using a painted back cloth of surrealistic design, or with strange, indefinable shapes set against a weirdly lit cyclorama. However elaborate the setting, it must be remembered that it vanishes in a black-out, and we are magically transported back to the tranquil Village Green. I am confident your ingenious back stage crew and effects team will achieve this minor miracle with spectacular results!

LIGHTING AND EFFECTS

During the action, all the main characters in this story are magically made to "disappear". Consequently, this means that quite a few flashes, followed by complete black-outs, are required to create this illusion. The other elements required are: loud thunder claps, unearthly sounds, dramatic and romantic lighting changes. General lighting for the Village Green, Country road and Farmyard scenes should be bright and sunny. Moonlight effect in Act I, Scene 5. Thunder claps and sinister lighting is required for when Mefisto conjures up his evil forces. There is an opportunity for some really bizarre and spooky lighting in The Place of the Disappeared (Act II, Scene 5) This should appear to be constantly changing, giving the place an unreal and nightmarish quality. Weird background noises and controlled ground mist will add to the eerie atmosphere. The use of follow spots for songs, individual characters and audience participation business is left to the director. An off stage microphone is required for the "voice" in the show tent (Act I, Scene 3)

MEFISTO'S MAGIC ACT

If he doesn't already have them, the actor playing Mefisto will need to acquire a few skills in the art of conjuring. These he displays to the crowd in the Show Tent (Act I, Scene 3), using conventional stage magician's props. They do not need to be elaborate conjuring tricks, but Mefisto must appear to perform them with great confidence and panache. They can be learnt from any good instruction book, or from your friendly neighbourhood magician!

THE ALTERNATIVE ACT

In the same scene, (Act I, Scene 3) there is a sequence in which the Duo, Fanny and Wally exchange corny gags. This can be played as scripted, or by using your own choice of gags. Alternatively, an "Act" can be substituted for this sequence. (This is at the discretion of the director.) It will depend on what competent local talent you may have available, and who is willing to perform for you — hopefully free! It can be a juggler, a contortionist, an instrumentalist, or even a fire eater! Please avoid singing and dancing, and certainly not a magic act. If you are inundated with local talent, it could be a different act for every performance! It will be necessary for Cindy Sparkle to announce "the act", using the performer/s real name/s or an invented one. After which, she and the Duo exit.

The time is Pantotime. This means that the style of settings and costumes can be a fantastical mixture of all periods.

Paul Reakes

Other works by Paul Reakes
published by Samuel French Ltd

Pantomimes

Babes in the Wood
Bluebeard
Cinderella
Dick Turpin
Goody Two Shoes
King Arthur
King Humpty Dumpty
Little Jack Horner
Little Miss Muffet
Little Red Riding Hood
Little Tommy Tucker
Old Mother Hubbard
Robinson Crusoe and the Pirates
Santa in Space
Sinbad the Sailor
Tom Thumb

Plays

Bang, You're Dead!
Mantrap

ACT I

SCENE 1

The Village Green

The back cloth shows picturesque countryside with Fanny's farm in the distance. The side wings represent quaint cottages, shops, an old inn and trees. Entrances at the back and R and L

The Chorus, Dancers and Children, as Villagers, are discovered. They go straight into a lively song and dance

Song 1

After the number, Fanny Fairacre enters from R

Fanny (*greeting the Villagers, warmly*) Morning, everybody!
Villagers Morning, Fanny!

The Villagers drift out in various directions

Fanny (*spotting the audience*) Oooh! Look! We've got visitors! (*Coming forward and greeting them*) Hello!

A few replies from the audience

Oh, come on! You can't have dozed off *already!* I said — (*yelling*) — HELLO!!

The audience shout back

That's better. I'm Fanny, Fanny Fairacre. I bet you can't guess what *I* am. (*By-play with the audience*) Ooh! You cheeky so-and-so! And I'm not a Lady Gaga look-a-like either! No. (*Proudly*) *I* have a smallholding! (*To someone*) You wouldn't think I had a smallholding to look at me, would you, dear? Well, I have. Hands up all those who want to see my smallholding! (*To someone*) *Hands*, dear! It's those bony things on the end of your arms. (*By-play with the audience*) Good! There it is! (*She goes up and points to the farm on the back cloth*) That's my smallholding! My lovely little farm. Nice, isn't it? (*Coming back down*) Eh? Why, what did *you* think my smallholding was, young man? Ooo! The minds of some people! You're not from [local place], are yah? I've heard they're a very strange lot there. I'm also a widow, by the way. Ahhh! (*She sighs and encourages them to join in*) No, I've been a widow much longer than that! (*She gets them to sigh again*) I run the farm with my son Freddie. Oh, he's a lovely lad. He's such a help to me. And good looking! Oh! He makes [current heart-throb] look like Shrek!

Freddie (*off* R, *calling*) Mum!
Fanny That's him now! Oh, girls! You won't be able to control yourselves when you see him.

Gormless and scruffy, Wally enters from R

Fanny He's so handsome and debonair. Just like a young Roger Moore! (*Or some other suave male personality*)
Wally Marnin'!
Fanny (*turning and reacting*) Eh?! You're not Freddie!
Wally Oi know oi bain't! (*Proudly*) Oi be a Wally!
Fanny You can say that again! (*To the audience*) This is Wally. He's a yokel local. He works for me on the farm.
Wally Ar! Oi be the pig boy!
Fanny They can see that! Or *smell* it! (*Holding her nose*) Phew! Have you been sleeping in that pig sty again?
Wally Ar!
Fanny That's not right, y'know. It's not healthy.
Wally Oi be all right.
Fanny I don't care about *you!* It's the *pigs* I'm worried about!

Handsome young Freddie Fairacre enters from R

Freddie Hello, Mum!
Fanny Ah! Here he is! My son Freddie. (*She puts her arm around Freddie and leads him forward. To the audience*) Well? What d'you think? Isn't he gorgeous! I bet you wish you had a son like him.
Wally (*to the audience, archly*) Oi bet you'd be worried if you did!
Fanny He takes after his mummy. He's got my eyes, my delicate features and my fabulous figure.
Wally Oi know *one* thing he ain't got!
Fanny (*suspiciously*) And what's that?
Wally Your legs!

Fanny (*looking at Freddie's legs*) No. He got those on eBay! I've just been telling these folk what a good son you are, Freddie.

Freddie Thanks, Mum.

Fanny Well, say hello. They won't bite. I think most of 'em have left their teeth at home.

Freddie (*to the audience*) Hello.

Fanny Oh, you'll have to try harder than that, son. (*In a stage whisper*) Some are from [local place].

Freddie (*louder*) Hello!

Audience Hello!

Wally (*pushing in*) 'Ere! Oi wanna say 'ello as well.

Fanny I think they've already got your drift. Phew! Oh, go on then!

Wally (*to the audience*) 'Ello!

Audience Hello!

Wally 'Ello again!

Audience Hello again!

Wally (*to Fanny*) Oi thinks they likes oi!

Fanny That's because you're up here, and they're down there! I've been telling them about the farm, Freddie.

Freddie (*to the audience*) Are you interested in farming? Do you like animals?

Wally (*pointing someone out*) *That* one does! Look who she's with!

Freddie We've got all sorts of livestock on our farm, haven't we, Mum?

Fanny Oh, yes! We've got the lot. We've got sheep, horses, chickens, pigs, geese! And what's that *other* one?

Wally Cows! That's the *UDDER* one! (*He guffaws*)

Fanny Oy! *I* do the jokes!

Wally Let us know when.

Freddie The farm's been in our family for generations.

Fanny Oh, yes! Since time immoral. Right back to my great-great grandfather. You might have heard of him. His name was Old Macdonald. And there's a song about him. (*Archly*) As if you didn't know!

Song 2

Song for Fanny, Freddie, Wally and the audience

Fanny Come on. We'd better get back to the farm.

Freddie If it's all right with you, Mum, I'd like to wait here for a while.

Fanny Don't tell me! (*Nudging him*) You're hoping to see Little Bo-Peep, aren't yah?

Freddie (*embarrassed*) Well ... I ... yes.
Fanny Ooh! Look at him blush.
Wally Ar! He's got a face like a slapped ——
Fanny That'll do! Of course you can wait to see Bo-Peep, Freddie. Who am I to stand in the way of love's young dream.
Wally No, that'd be a nightmare!
Fanny I'm warnin' you!
Freddie She should be along with her sheep anytime now. I'll only be with her for a little bit.
Fanny (*to Wally, warningly*) Don't even think about it! (*To Freddie*) See you later then. (*To Wally*) Come on, Aroma! Haven't you got some piggies to pamper?
Wally 'Ere! What do you give a pig with chilblains?
Fanny I dunno.
Wally O*ink*ment! (*He guffaws*)
Fanny (*to the audience*) You'll have to forgive him, folks. His father spent a lot of time in [local place]! (*Pushing him out* R) Get out! (*To the audience, waving*) See you later! Bye!

Fanny and Wally exit

Freddie (*to the audience*) Mum was right when she called it love's young dream. Because I really do love Bo-Peep. I love her with all my heart.

Song 3

Romantic song for Freddie with romantic lighting

The Villagers enter and join in the refrain

After the number, the lighting returns to normal

Arrogant and haughty Lady Sneering enters at the back. She pushes her way through the Villagers

Lady S Stand aside! Out of my way, you common clodhoppers! Stand aside!
Freddie (*moving to her*) Good-morning. Can I help you?
Lady S (*taking in his handsome face and form, and liking what she sees*) Yes ... Oh, yes, you certainly can! (*Aside*) What a handsome hunk of humanity! (*Recovering her haughty pose*) *I* am Lady Sneering. I have just taken up residence at Moneybags Manor.
Freddie (*with an elegant bow*) Your ladyship.

Lady S (*aside*) How supple he is! I must get to know him better. (*To Freddie*) And you are?
Freddie Freddie Fairacre of Fairacre Farm. Can I be of any assistance?
Lady S (*aside*) And nice manners too, for a commoner. (*To Freddie*) I am unfamiliar with this rustic backwater. I require the assistance of someone who will take me on a guided tour of this *revolting* village and its *sordid* surroundings. You will do nicely, Freddie Fairacre! (*Aside*) Very nicely indeed!
Freddie It will be my pleasure.
Lady S We will leave at once. (*Moving closer to him*) I will allow you to take my arm ... Freddie.
Freddie Oh! Do you mean right away?
Lady S Of course! Why not?
Freddie I'm afraid it's not convenient at the moment.
Lady S Why not? If *I* command it!
Freddie I'm meeting someone.
Lady S Pah! Put them off.
Freddie I don't want to do that. It's someone very special.
Lady S Someone more special than a member of your aristocracy?
Freddie Yes. You see ... it's the girl I love.
Lady S (*reacting*) The girl you love! (*Scornfully*) Pah! Some common village wench no doubt.
Freddie She is far from common, I assure you. (*He looks towards* R *entrance*) Why, here she comes now. You can judge for yourself.

Little Bo-Peep enters from R. *She is petite, pretty and charmingly dressed in shepherdess costume. She carries a shepherd's crook*

Bo-Peep (*greeting all with a radiant smile*) Good-morning, everyone.
Villagers Morning, Bo-Peep!

Freddie crosses to Bo-Peep. He takes her hands and gazes adoringly at her. Lady Sneering is not happy, to say the least!

Freddie Hello, Bo.
Bo-Peep Hello, Freddie.

They gaze adoringly into each other's eyes. Lady Sneering gives an impatient cough

Lady S Hhhhm!!
Freddie (*coming down to earth*) Oh, yes! Bo, there's someone I'd like you to meet. (*Indicating the audience*) These are some new friends of mine.

Lady S (*greatly affronted. To the audience*) Well really! Introducing you common trash before *me!*
Freddie (*to the audience*) This is Bo-Peep.
Bo-Peep (*greeting them*) Hello, everybody!
Audience Hello, Bo-Peep.
Bo-Peep (*to Freddie*) They're very nice, aren't they?
Freddie Yes. Even the ones from [local place].
Bo-Peep Oh, I went there once, but it was shut.
Lady S (*by now very annoyed*) How much longer am I to be kept waiting?
Freddie Oh, yes! There's someone else. (*He leads Bo-Peep over to Lady Sneering*) Lady Sneering, allow me to present Miss Bo-Peep.
Bo-Peep Your ladyship. (*She does a very neat curtsy*)
Lady S (*pronouncing it with disdain*) Bo-Peep! Is that really your name?
Bo-Peep Yes.
Lady S (*with a scornful laugh*) Ha! How utterly absurd and ridiculous. It's a very stupid name. (*To the audience*) Isn't it?
Audience No!
Lady S Oh, yes, it is!
Audience Oh, no, it isn't!

This continues ad-lib

Lady S Well, I don't really care what *you* think! (*With venom*) You're just a collection of common clodhoppers! A pack of pathetic peasants. (*To the Villagers*) Out of my way! Stand aside!

The Villagers part

Lady Sneering sweeps out at the back

The Villagers exit in various directions

Bo-Peep That wasn't very nice. I know Bo-Peep *is* an odd sort of name, but I can't help what I'm called.
Freddie (*smiling*) Of course you can't. (*Taking her hand*) Anyway, one day soon I hope to change your name to mine.
Bo-Peep Oh, Freddie! Do you mean it?
Freddie Yes. That's if you'll have me.
Bo-Peep Of course I will.

Freddie and Bo-Peep embrace

The loud "Baa-ing" of sheep is heard from off R

Bo-Peep Oh, it's the sheep! They get very jealous, you know. (*Going to* R *and calling to off stage*) It's all right. I haven't forgotten you. You can stop now.

The sheep sounds stop abruptly

Freddie (*to the audience*) They're very well behaved sheep, aren't they? Bo-Peep's a wonderful shepherd.
Bo-Peep (*to the audience*) Would you like to see my flock?
Freddie (*to someone*) She means her *sheep!*
Audience Yes!
Bo-Peep Are you sure?
Audience Yes!
Bo-Peep All right. I'll go and fetch them.

Bo-Peep exits R

Freddie (*to the audience*) I must warn you. This is a very, very *rare* breed of sheep. You've probably never seen sheep like *these* before — anywhere.

Song 4

To suitable music, the sheep (Children) enter in single file from R, *with Bo-Peep following behind them*

Bo-Peep sings. This is followed by a dance routine for the sheep, with Bo-Peep and Freddie joining in. It ends in a tableau

Freddie (*to the audience*) Wasn't that great? They're really clever sheep, aren't they? I bet they all went to [local school/college]!
Sheep (*bleating, loudly*) Baa! Baa!

Fanny enters from L

Fanny What's all the racket about?
Freddie It's just the sheep, Mum.
Fanny Oh, good. I thought it was the [local reference] bleating about something again. (*Petting the sheep*) Hello, my lovelies, hello! How's my little woolly wonders today?
Sheep Baa! Baa!

Fanny Oh, I'm pleased to hear that. (*To the audience*) They're lovely, aren't they? Almost human! It's odd, though. They've all got the same name. I bet you can't guess what it is? (*By-play with the audience*) No! It's — *Baaa*sil! (*One of the sheep gives her a nudge*) Looks like *they've* heard that one before as well! I must say you're doin' a grand job, Bo-Peep. Our last shepherd was hopeless with the sheep.
Bo-Peep Why?
Fanny He kept fallin' asleep countin' em! Where are you takin' 'em now?
Bo-Peep To graze in the meadow.
Freddie (*to Bo-Peep*) I'll come with you.
Fanny I thought you might! And don't you two get up to anything. Those sheep tell me everything, y'know!

Bo-Peep and Freddie herd the sheep off at the back

Comic business as Fanny has to round up a stray one and guide it out after the others

Fanny (*to the audience*) As you all liked my Baasil joke so much, I'll tell you another one. What do you get if you cross a sheep with a radiator? Give up? *Central bleating!* Get it? Oh, please yourselves!

The beat of a drum and the clash of cymbals is heard off R

The Villagers enter at the back and L. Ding and Dong march on from R. Ding beats a drum. Dong follows behind, clashing a pair of cymbals

Ding and Dong parade around the stage. Ding comes to sudden halt and Dong crashes into him and falls over. Comic business as Ding, hampered by the drum, tries to help Dong to his feet. Eventually, they sort themselves out

Ding (*conscious the others are watching them*) Go on! Say something! They're all looking at us!
Dong (*to the audience*) Hi, there! How's it goin'? Are you all right?
Ding Not to *them!* To the gathered populace!
Dong The whatulace?
Ding (*indicating the Villagers*) Them! *You* start it, remember!
Dong Oh, yeah! (*He clears his throat and announces grandly*) Ladels and jelly spoons!
Ding We are here to announce the arrival of ...
Dong The amazing!
Ding The fabulous!
Dong The sensational!

Ding The spectacular!
Dong } *(together) Cindy Sparkle!*
Ding

They loudly beat the drum and clash the cymbals

> *Glittering Cindy Sparkle sweeps on from* R. *She does a twirl and strikes a flamboyant pose*

Fanny comes down to Ding and Dong, who are still making a racket

Fanny Oy! Oy! Cut it out! *Cut it out!*

Ding and Dong stop

> That's enough of that! We'll all end up with percolated eardrums! *(She goes to Cindy)*

Cindy is still holding the pose. Fanny looks her up and down, and then turns to Ding and Dong

> D'you mind telling us what [politician] is doin' here?
Ding You see before you, the one and only ...
Dong } *(together, with showbiz razzmatazz gestures) CindySparkle!*
Ding

Cindy does a twirl and strikes another flamboyant pose

Fanny *(to the audience)* Crikey! Those Duracells are good, aren't they? *(To Cindy)* Look, dear, give your engine a rest, and tell us what's goin' on.
Cindy *(dropping her pose and addressing the crowd in a grand manner)* Ladies and gentlemen! Your attention, if you please! *I* am Cindy Sparkle! Cindy Sparkle of Sparkle's sparklingly spectacular!
Fanny *(to the audience)* Try sayin' that after you've had a few.
Cindy Allow me to present the highly versatile ... *(she indicates Ding and Dong)* ... Ding and Dong!

Ding and Dong perform a comic bow

Fanny Were they born like that, or did they have to take lessons?
Cindy We have pitched our tent on the other side of your village.
Fanny I hope you've got permission from [local reference]. Oh, I get it. You're some sort of travelling show.

Cindy (*grandly*) We are the *show of shows!* And for a modest fee, it will
be our great pleasure and privilege to present all manner of entrancing
entertainments! We have singing!

Ding } (*together, deadpan*) Tra la la! Tra la la!
Dong

Cindy Dancing!

Ding and Dong perform a very short dance

Cindy Comedy!
Ding I say, I say, I say! My dog's got no nose!
Dong Your dog's got no nose? How does he smell?
Ding Horrible!
Fanny You've got that bit right! (*To the audience*) Simon Cowell would
have a field day with this lot! (*To Cindy*) And you're asking us to pay
good money to see *this?*
Cindy Just a mere trifle.
Fanny I don't care if it's just a tiny blancmange! I wouldn't pay a penny
to see those two no-hopers!
Ding There's not only *us*.
Dong There's others as well.
Fanny Don't tell me you've brought [current performer] with yah!
Cindy There is also our sensational main attraction. The mighty Mefisto!
Fanny Who's he when he's at home?
Cindy Mefisto is the greatest magician who has ever lived!
Fanny (*scoffing*) Oh, yeah! And I'm Britney Spears!
Dong (*shaking her hand*) Oh, hello! I've always wanted to meet you! I
must say, you're a lot bigger in the flesh.
Fanny Ger off! (*To Cindy*) Where is this mighty Misfit, or whatever his
name is?

There is a flash

The sinister figure of Mefisto appears from L

All react

Fanny Crikey! It's [someone topical to suit]!
Cindy (*to all*) Allow me to present — the mighty Mefisto! The world's
greatest magician!
Fanny (*moving to him*) So! You do tricks, do yah?
Mefisto (*with disdain*) *Tricks!* I am no common conjurer! (*Grandly*) *I*
am a true follower of the black arts!
Fanny I'm a [football team] supporter meself.

Mefisto My cabalistic capabilities are enormous!
Fanny I bet you say that to all the girls.
Mefisto Do you wish me to display my attributes?
Fanny No, thanks! I've got a weak stomach! Just show us some magic.
Mefisto Very well. I will ask you to think of a person. Any person you choose. With my mighty magical powers I will transport that person to this very spot.
Fanny Anyone I like? And you'll bring 'em right here?
Mefisto Yes.
Fanny Let me think ... er ... (*To the audience*) How about [current male heart-throb]! No, better not. We don't want Gran to get *too* excited, do we? (*To Mefisto*) All right! I've thought of someone. Wally, my pig boy! Bring *him* here.
Mefisto So be it! (*He raises his arms*)
                    I summon the powers of sorcery!
                    Come to my aid and work for me!

There is a great crash of thunder. The lighting becomes dark and sinister. All react

                    Wally, the pig boy, wherever you may be,
                    I command you come here — for all to see!

There is a flash. The lighting returns to normal

Wally appears from L. His trousers are down around his ankles and he is holding a roll of toilet paper. He looks confused, to say the least!

Wally 'Ere! Wos goin' on?! Oi was in the ... (*He looks down at his trousers and gulps*) OH, ERH.

The others laugh

Highly embarrassed, Wally shuffles out L, as fast as his dropped trousers will allow him

Mefisto (*to Fanny, pompously*) Well? Does that prove I am the greatest magician in the whole world?
Fanny It does! You certainly caught him with his trousers down.
Cindy (*to all*) And that was only a small example of Mefisto's mighty power. Come to our show this afternoon and you will witness many more miraculous marvels. The entertainment commences at two-thirty! Bring all your friends! For the time being, I bid you all — farewell!

Cindy makes a flamboyant bow, and then exits L. *Ding and Dong march out after her, banging the drum and clashing the cymbals. The Villagers exit in various directions*

Mefisto is about to leave, but Fanny stops him

Fanny Just a minute, Mr Misshape. D'you think you could do me a *personal* favour with your magic?
Mefisto What is it?

Fanny looks about, then whispers in his ear. He looks her up and down

Even *my* magical power has its limits! Ha! Ha! Ha!

Laughing his unpleasant laugh, Mefisto sweeps out L

Fanny Flippin' cheek! I only asked him if he could make me look like [current model]! That shouldn't be difficult, should it? All right! There's no need to take a vote on it!

Fanny exits L. *Freddie and Bo-Peep enter from* R, *holding hands*

Song 5

Romantic duet with romantic lighting

During the dance break, Lady Sneering enters downstage. She observes the couple with obvious displeasure. She stamps her foot in annoyance, and storms out

The lovers resume the song to its conclusion. They embrace.

The Lights fade to Black-out. Music to cover the scene change

SCENE 2

Near the farm

Tabs, or a front cloth showing a picturesque country road. Entrances DR *and* DL

Lady Sneering enters DL. *She is seething with rage and takes it out on the audience*

Lady S So! You are still here, are you? You ragged rabble of revolting riff raff! (*By-play with the audience*) *What!* How dare you! How dare you show disrespect to a person of my noble rank and breeding! I can have you all thrown out of here, if I choose! None of you are fit to clean my shoes. No more is that wretched girl with the ridiculous name. *Bo-Peep!* Pah! What could handsome Freddie Fairacre possibly want with *her* when he could have *me!* *I* who have everything! Great wealth, exquisite beauty, excessive charm, and the best manicure that [local beauty salon] can provide. Well, let me tell you this, you putrid peasants. I mean to have Freddie Fairacre for myself! Oh, yes! And no mealy-mouthed little shepherdess is going to stop me! I always get what I want! And I will this time! Oh, yes, I will!

Audience Oh, no, you won't!

Lady S Oh, yes, I will!

This continues ad-lib

Pah! Take my word for it, you tatty trash! Soon Freddie Fairacre and Little Bo-Peep will no longer be an item! Ha! Ha! Ha!

Laughing her sneering laugh, she exits DR

Cindy enters DL. *She no longer has her showbiz sparkle, but looks worried and troubled. Ding and Dong follow her on at a distance, watching her with concern*

Ding Cindy looks very down in the dumps.

Dong Yeah. You'd think we were in [local place].

Ding Go and ask her what's wrong. You've got a sympathetic ear.

Dong I've got a runny nose as well. Let's both ask her.

Ding (*as they move to her*) Cindy, are you worried about something?

Cindy (*turning to them, still distracted*) It's ... It's nothing.

Ding Come on. You can tell us.

Dong Yeah. I've got a synthetic ear.

Cindy Well, if you must know ... it's Mefisto. He's asking for more money.

Ding What! He already gets more than the rest of us put together.

Cindy I know. But he's threatening to leave the show if I don't increase his salary.

Dong Tell him to take a long walk off a short pier!

Cindy I'd love to. He's not my favourite person. But he is a tremendous draw. People come just to see his magic. I hate to admit it, but without Mefisto we'd go out of business.

Ding What are you going to do?

Cindy (*sighing*) I really don't know.
Ding We'll go without our wages, if it'll help. Won't we, Dong?
Dong Yeah! We'll perform free and lettuce.
Ding And I'll talk to the rest of the troupe. I'm sure they'll take a drop in pay to save the show.
Dong Even if it does mean keeping murky Mefisto around.
Cindy Thanks, boys. But it won't make any difference. Everyone is working for next to nothing as it is. I'd love to pay you all better wages, but it's just not possible. So even if you all agreed to work for nothing, it wouldn't solve the problem. Thanks for the offer anyway. (*She puts her arms around them and smiles for the first time*)
Ding That's better! We don't like to see you looking so miserable.
Dong No! Remember who you are! You're the one and only ...
Ding ⎫
Dong ⎭ (*together, with big razzmatazz gestures*) ... Cindy Sparkle!

Song 6

Song and dance routine for Ding, Dong and Cindy

After the number, Cindy kisses them both on the cheek and exits DR

Ding moves to the exit, watching her departure

Ding (*moving away from the exit*) That rotten Mefisto! He's got Cindy right over a barrel!
Dong (*rushing to the exit*) Eh?! (*Looking off*) I can't see him! ... *Or a barrel!*
Ding You twit! I was speaking metaphorically.
Dong Ooh! Get you! (*To the audience*) He's swallowed the dictionary again!
Ding Cindy's in a dilemma.
Dong I thought you said she was in a barrel!
Ding If she doesn't pay Mefisto, he'll leave the show and she'll be forced to close down. We'll all lose our livelihoods.
Dong Oh, I never wear hoods! They make me look like a tortoise! (*He demonstrates*)
Ding I wish there was something we could do to help.
Dong I know! Let's buy Mefisto a one way ticket to [local place]!
Ding D'you know, you're two steps from an idiot?
Dong Am I? I'll move then. (*He does so and giggles*)
Ding Stop messing about! This is serious!
Dong I know it is! It's even more serious than [current situation on TV soap]! But what can *we* do about it? Like you said, he's got Cindy over a barrel and in a diploma.

Ding All we can do is show him how we feel about him.
Dong Yeah!
Ding We'll show him contempt!
Dong Yeah!
Ding We'll show him disdain!
Dong Yeah! (*Doing a double take*) *What* stain?
Ding We'll tell him he's a rotten old twister!
Dong Yeah!
Ding And if he doesn't like it, you can thump him!
Dong Yeah! (*Doing a double take*) Eh? *I'm* not thumping him! He might use his magic powers on us. He might turn us into [topical reference], or something horrible like that!
Ding That's true. The best thing to do is keep out of his way.
Dong Yeah. We'll get our mates out there to warn us if they see him. (*To the audience*) You'll do that, won't you?
Audience Yes!
Ding (*to the audience*) You'll give a shout if you see him, won't you?
Audience Yes!
Dong Great! (*To Ding*) They're very friendly, aren't they?
Ding They are. Especially the ones over there. (*He points out a group*)

While they are thus engaged, Mefisto enters DL

The audience shouts out warnings. Mefisto moves to behind the duo

Ding (*to the audience*) What's that?
Dong Is it him?
Audience Yes!
Ding Are you sure?
Audience Yes!
Dong Where is he?
Audience Behind you!
Ding Behind us?
Audience Yes!
Dong Is he really?
Audience Yes!
Ding (*to Dong, nervously*) We'd better take a look!

Comic business as they nervously turn around with Mefisto keeping behind them

Duo (*as they face the back*) No, he's not! Where is he now?
Audience Behind you!

16   Little Bo-Peep

They repeat the turning business

Duo (*as they face the front*) No, he's not!
Ding I think they're having us on.
Dong Yeah! Stop playing tricks on us!

Mefisto steps from behind them and stands close to Dong

(*To Mefisto, casually*) Oh, there you are. That lot said you were *behind* us, and ——
Mefisto (*raising his arms and giving his demonic laugh*) Ha! Ha! Ha!

Yelling, Ding and Dong run out DR

(*To the audience*) Those two fools! They are almost as stupid as you are! And I know you are all stupid because *I* am the mighty Mefisto! With my magical powers I know everything! For instance! I know that *you* ... (*he points to someone*) ... pick your nose when you think no one is looking! And *you* ... (*he points to someone else*) ... no! It's too *disgusting* to repeat what *you* do! No secret is safe from the mighty Mefisto! Ha! Ha! Ha! Despite *your* obnoxious presence here, I quite like this neighbourhood. I would rather like to buy a house at [local "Posh" area]! When Cindy Sparkle raises my salary, I shall be able to afford one. I'm sure you'll love having me live near you! I'll have great fun trying out some of my most diabolical magic on you little worms! Oh, yes, I will!
Audience Oh, no, you won't!
Mefisto Oh, yes, I will!

This continues ad-lib

It ends with Mefisto sweeping off stage, laughing his evil laugh

The Lights fade to black-out

Loud, brassy "Showbiz" style music is played to cover the scene change. This continues, as the Lights come up on —

SCENE 3

In the show tent

The back cloth and side wings represent the colourful interior of a show tent. Across the back is a raised platform with benches for the spectators.

There are smaller single benches DR *and* DL. *The entrance to the tent is* R.
An entrance for the performers is L

*The brash "Showbiz" music continues to play as the Villagers are seen
entering the tent from* R. *Ding is taking the money. Dong is showing
people to the seats at the back. When all the Villagers are seated, Freddie
and Bo-Peep enter from* R. *They pay, and are shown to the bench* DR,
where they sit. Lady Sneering makes a grand entrance from R. *She pays,
grudgingly, and is shown to a seat at the back. She looks at the Villagers
with revulsion and seats herself on the bench* DL. *The Duo exit* L. *Lady
Sneering sees the two lovers sitting opposite her. She gets up and crosses
to them. She sits very close to Freddie, forcing Bo-Peep to budge up*

The music comes to an end. An expectant hush falls. A fanfare sounds

Voice (*from off stage microphone*) Ladies and gentlemen! Welcome to
  Cindy Sparkle's sparkling spectacular! A show that is guaranteed to
  give you the thrill of a lifetime! And so, without further ado, strike up
  the band and let the show — *begin!*

Suitable music strikes up

  Ding and Dong march on from L

*They parade around the stage, waving flamboyantly to the Villagers and
audience. As before, Ding comes to a sudden halt, and Dong crashes
into him and falls over. Ding helps him up, and they both bow to the
Villagers and audience. The music stops*

Ding (*grandly*) Ladies and gentlemen!
Dong And kiddiewinkies!
Ding The first item on today's programme is ...

  Fanny and Wally rush on from R

Fanny Has it started? Has it started? (*Spotting the audience and waving
  to them*) Oh! Hello, folks! You got here before us then. What have we
  missed? Is it any good?
Ding Excuse me. I was just about to pontificate.
Fanny You can get arrested for that!
Dong You're late!
Fanny I know! I wanted to watch the end of *Flog It* [or other daytime
  antique programme]. (*To the audience*) I love all those dusty old
  relics.

Wally She likes to see the competition! (*He guffaws*)
Fanny *You'll* see my fist in a minute! (*To Ding and Dong*) Well, we're
'ere now! You can get on with it!
Ding Have you paid?
Fanny How much is it?
Ding Fifty pence each.
Fanny A pound! I haven't got a pound on me. (*To Wally, with a nudge*)
Have you?
Wally No, no oi ain't! (*He winks and goes to Dong*) 'Ere! Can you lend
oi a pound?
Dong Of course! (*He digs in his pocket and gives Wally a coin*) A pound.
Wally Ta! (*He goes to Fanny and gives her the coin*) A pound.
Fanny Ta! (*She goes to Ding and gives him the coin*) A pound.

*Fanny returns to Wally. They chuckle together. Ding and Dong look at
each other in puzzlement*

Dong (*to Fanny*) Hey! Just a minute ...
Fanny Come on! Get this show on the road!

Fanny and Wally sit on the bench DL

Ding (*to all, announcing*) The first item on today's programme is —
Cindy Sparkle and the Dancing Dainties!

Gesturing to L, *Ding and Dong clear to stage* R. *Music starts*

Cindy, arrayed in another glittering costume, sweeps on from L. *She
does a twirl and strikes a pose*

Fanny (*to the audience*) She's at it again!

A troupe of shapely female Dancers trip on from L. *They do twirls and
strike poses*

(*To the audience*) Crikey! It must be catching!

Cindy and the Dancers go into their song and dance routine

Song 7

*The number ends with a flamboyant finish and pose. The spectators cheer
and applaud. Wally gets up and goes to shake hands with Cindy. Fanny
drags him back to his seat. Cindy and the Dancers break their pose*

The Dancers trip off L

Cindy (*addressing the crowd*) And now, ladies and gentlemen! Are you ready for more titillation?
Wally (*jumping up with great enthusiasm*) ARH!
Fanny (*pulling him down*) Behave yerself! You're not at the [local pub or club] now!
Cindy (*to the crowd*) Then prepare to be thrilled by the amazing — *Ding and Dong!* (*Or alternative act*)

NOTE: For alternative act instead of the following sequence see Production Note

Fanny Oh, no! it's Wallace and Gromit again!
Ding I say, I say, I say! What do you get if you pour hot water down a rabbit hole?
Dong I don't know. What *do* you get?
Ding *Hot cross bunnies!*
Dong I say, I say, I say! Why was the Egyptian girl worried?
Ding I don't know. Why *was* she worried?
Dong Because her *Daddy* was a *Mummy!*
Ding What do you call a woman with two toilets on her head?
Dong I don't know. What *do* you call her?
Ding *Lu-lu!*
Dong What do you call ...
Fanny (*jumping up*) Hold it! Hold it! That's terrible! I've heard better jokes on *Songs of Praise!*
Wally (*standing*) Ar! They be rubbish!
Ding Well, if you two think you can do any better ...!
Fanny We can! Out the way!

Fanny and Wally push Ding and Dong aside and take centre stage

Fanny I say, I say, I say! What kind of instrument does a fisherman play?
Wally I don't know. What *does* a fisherman play?
Fanny A *cast-a-net!*
Wally I say, I say, I say! What do your call a pig with no clothes on?
Fanny I don't know. What *do* you call a pig with no clothes on?
Wally *Streaky bacon!*
Fanny Why did the farmer plough his field with a steamroller?
Wally I don't know. Why did he?
Fanny Because he wanted to grow *mashed potatoes!*
Wally What do you get if ...
Ding Hey! Hey! Those jokes are just as bad as ours!

Fanny What d'you mean! Our jokes are far better than yours!

Ding ⎫
Dong ⎭ (*together*) Oh, no, they're not!

Fanny ⎫
Wally ⎭ (*together*) Oh, yes, they are!

This continues. Each pair encourages the Villagers and the audience to take sides

When the noisy argument is at its height, Cindy hurries on and takes control

Fanny and Wally return to their bench

Cindy, Ding and Dong exit L

NOTE: If an alternative act is used, the Villagers applaud

"The Act" takes a bow, and exits L

Voice (*from off stage microphone*) Ladies and gentlemen! The moment has arrived! The moment you have all been waiting for! The man you are about to see is a legend in his own lifetime! He has mystified many millions with his miraculous magic! Prepare to be amazed! Prepare to be mesmerized! Prepare to meet — the mighty Mefisto!

There is a flash

Mefisto appears. He bows to the awestruck spectators

Fanny (*to the audience*) Look out! [Politician]'s back!

Mefisto claps his hands together

Don't start clapping! You haven't done anything yet!

The Duo enter from L. *They carry a small table, draped in a black cloth decorated with magical symbols. On the table are various items used by Mefisto in his act. They place the table* DC, *and exit* L

Mefisto moves behind the table

(*To the audience*) Oh, no! Not another flippin' cookery programme!

Suitable "mysterious" music plays. Mefisto goes into his act. Using the items on the table, he performs a few conventional magic tricks. (See Production Notes.) At its conclusion, he steps away from the table and takes a bow. The spectators applaud

The Duo enter L, *and quickly remove the table*

The "mysterious" music stops

(*Unimpressed*) That was a bit old hat! Why don't you do something *really* amazing. Like what you did to Wally.

Wally 'E won't catch oi out again. (*To the audience with a chortle*) Oi went before oi come!

Mefisto So! You wish to see more of my *special* powers, do you?

Fanny That's why we're 'ere! Give us some of the good stuff!

Mefisto Very well! So be it! (*Turning to the spectators*) First, I shall require the assistance of a volunteer. (*He looks around*) A beautiful young woman, perhaps?

Fanny (*preening herself*) Oooh! Is he looking at *me?*

Wally Ar! He should've gone to Specsavers!

Mefisto (*approaching Lady Sneering*) *You*, perhaps?

Lady S Certainly not!

Mefisto (*moving to Bo-Peep*) Perhaps *you?*

Bo-Peep (*unsure*) Well, I ...

Mefisto I assure you, there is nothing to fear. Your name?

Bo-Peep Bo-Peep. (*Standing up*) What do I have to do?

Mefisto Not a thing, *I* will do all that is required. (*He takes Bo-Peep by the hand and leads her to* C. *He raises his arms*)
I summon the powers of sorcery!
Come to my aid and work for me!

There is a great crash of thunder. The lighting becomes dark and sinister. All react

I command you, dark forces that inhabit the night,
Make Bo-Peep vanish, and disappear from sight!

He makes a magic pass at Bo-Peep. There is a flash, followed by a complete black-out

Bo-Peep exits

Startled cries from the spectators and Mefisto's laughter is heard in the darkness

The Lights return to normal. Bo-Peep has vanished from the scene. Consternation! Everyone leaps to their feet and looks about. Fanny and Wally start searching under their bench

Mefisto (*seeing them*) You will not find her there! You will not find her — *anywhere!* Ha! Ha! Ha!
Freddie (*rushing to Mefisto*) Where is she? What have you done with Bo-Peep? Bring her back at once!
Mefisto Ha! Ha! Ha!
Freddie (*grabbing Mefisto*) Bring her back, I say!
Mefisto Take your hands off me!

Cindy rushes on from L, *followed by Ding and Dong*

Cindy What's the problem?
Mefisto This young fool attacked me!
Freddie He made Bo-Peep disappear! And he's refusing to bring her back!
Cindy (*to Mefisto*) Is this true?
Mefisto I *did* make her disappear, yes. But I have *not* refused to bring her back.
Cindy Then kindly do so at once.
Others Yes! Bring her back! Go on!
Mefisto (*with a mocking bow*) Very well! (*He raises his arms*)
           I command you, dark forces that inhabit the night,
           Make Bo-Peep reappear, and return to our sight!

He makes a magic pass. There is a flash, followed by a complete Black-out

    Bo-Peep enters

The Lights return to normal. Bo-Peep is standing there. She looks about her, confused and frightened

Freddie Bo!
Bo-Peep (*rushing into his arms*) Oh, Freddie! I was so frightened! That ... that awful place!
Freddie Where did you go? (*To Mefisto*) Where did you send her?
Mefisto (*sneering*) To a place that is not very pleasant!
Fanny You never sent the poor girl to [local reference]!
Mefisto She went to — *The Place of the Disappeared!* A destination to which only *I* have the power to send people. And to bring them back — *if I choose!*

Freddie (*to Bo-Peep*) It's all right. You're safe now. (*To Mefisto*) And if you ever attempt anything like that again, I'll knock your block off!
Cindy (*to all*) Ladies and gentlemen! Will you please return to your seats for the rest of the show.
Fanny I don't want to see anymore. Old Misfit has put me right off! I'm goin' 'ome!

The Villagers voice their agreement and quickly file out on R

(*To Cindy*) Take my tip, dear. I'd replace *him* (*indicating Mefisto*) with Anne Robinson. She's more people friendly!

Fanny exits R, *taking Wally out with her*

Lady S Freddie, I wish to return to Moneybags Manor. You will escort me.
Freddie I'm *sorry, your* ladyship. Bo-Peep is still upset. I need to be with her. Come along, Bo.

Freddie leads Bo-Peep out R

Lady Sneering stamps her foot with rage. She gathers up her things and starts to put on her gloves

Cindy (*to Mefisto*) You went too far. You upset them. They'll never come back now.
Mefisto (*pompously*) They will always come back to see the mighty Mefisto! And that reminds me. Have you come to a decision about my raise in salary?
Cindy I've already told you. It's impossible to pay you any more.
Mefisto Then you leave me no alternative. I will resign from this miserable side show of yours.
Cindy But we'll go out of business!
Mefisto Quite true. The choice is yours. Increase my salary or I leave.
Cindy But there's no extra money!
Mefisto That's your problem. Try selling something. (*Indicating Ding and Dong*) These two halfwits, perhaps! I hear [topical/ local reference to suit] are looking for some replacements! Ha! Ha! Ha!

Mefisto sweeps out R. *Ding and Dong blow raspberries after him. On the verge of tears, Cindy runs out* L. *Ding and Dong run out after her*

Lady S (*to the audience*) That magician has given me an idea. He could help me get Freddie away from that nauseating Little Bo-Peep! If he

can make her disappear once, I am sure he can be persuaded to do so
again! Ha! Ha! Ha!

Laughing her unpleasant laugh, Lady Sneering sweeps out R

The Lights fade out

Music to cover the scene change

SCENE 4

Near the farm

Tabs, or front cloth as used in Act I, Scene 2

Wally enters from DL. *He is walking on air with a big soppy grin on his
face. Fanny follows him on*

Fanny Hey! What's up with you? Have you been at the wine gums
again?
Wally Oi be in love! (*He holds his chest and gives a groan*) Oooh!
Fanny Rubbish! That's heartburn! (*To the audience*) Anyone got some
Gaviscon?
Wally No, it bain't! It be love! (*Giving a big sigh*) Oh, Cindy Sparkle!
Oi luuuvyou!
Fanny Cindy Sparkle! D'you mean her with the (*she does a twirl*) and
the (*she does a pose*)?
Wally (*blissfully*) Ar!
Fanny Ha! You can forget that.
Wally Why?
Fanny Don't be a wally, Wally. She's well out of your league. She's
way above you.
Wally She bain't that tall!
Fanny (*to the audience*) If brains were dynamite, he wouldn't have
enough to blow his hat off with!
Wally Oi be gonna ask her out.
Fanny Where? Your idea of a good time is a bag of chips outside the
[local reference]!
Wally Oi be thinking of taking her to the [local "posh" restaurant] Oi
bet she'd like that.
Fanny Listen. I don't wish to be a wet blanket in the ointment, but she
might turn you down, y'know.

Wally Wull, you know the old sayin' — nothing ventured, nothing gained!
Fanny There's another old sayin' — you can't make a silk purse out of a sow's ear! And talking of pigs, we should be getting back to the farm. There's lots to do, and I'm getting a little behind.
Wally When's it arriving?
Fanny What?
Wally Your little behind! (*He guffaws*)
Fanny (*pushing him out* DR) *OUT!*

Wally exits

(*To the Audience*) He's got about as much chance of taking her out, as I've got of becoming the next [female personality]! On second thoughts, that's not so daft, is it? Oh! Don't take a vote again!

Fanny exits DR. *Freddie and Bo-Peep enter from* DL

Freddie How are you feeling now, Bo?
Bo-Peep Better, thanks.
Freddie Do you feel like talking about it?
Bo-Peep I suppose so.
Freddie Where did you go when Mefisto made you disappear?
Bo-Peep I don't really know. I was only there for a few seconds. (*She shivers at the memory*) But I *never want* to go back there again.
Freddie (*putting his arm around her*) What sort of place was it?
Bo-Peep I ... I can't really describe it. It was nightmarish ... horrible ... Oh, I don't want to talk about it anymore, Freddie.
Freddie Then we won't. Forget all about it. Let's talk about *us* instead.

Freddie and Bo-Peep exit DR

Or —

Reprise of Song 5 (Optional)

If more time is required for the scene change, Freddie and Bo-Peep can sing a short reprise of their love duet

After which, they exit DR

Mefisto enters from DL. *He sneers at the audience, and is about to exit* DR, *when Lady Sneering enters from* DL

Lady S (*calling to him*) You there!
Mefisto (*turning*) Who calls the mighty Mefisto?
Lady S I am Lady Sneering. Of Moneybags Manor.
Mefisto Moneybags *Manor!* What a *delightful* address. (*Moving to her*)
Your ladyship. (*He gives her a smarmy bow*) What can I do for you?
Lady S I require your services as a magician. (*Darkly*) Your *special*
services.
Mefisto With pleasure. But they don't come cheap.
Lady S You will be paid handsomely. *Very* handsomely. (*From her bag
she produces two big wads of bank notes*)

Mefisto eyes them greedily and rubs his hands

Mefisto I am yours to command, your ladyship. What do you require
of me?
Lady S (*after looking about to make sure they are alone*) I want you to
repeat what you did this afternoon.
Mefisto Ah! You wish me to give a private performance at Moneybags
Manor?
Lady S Certainly not! I want you to make Bo-Peep disappear again!
Only this time, you will *not* bring her back. I want you to make her
disappear — *permanently!* Do you understand?
Mefisto Indeed I do, your ladyship. It will not be a problem. (*With an
evil chuckle*) I have done it many times before. There have been those
in the past who have displeased me, and they have never been seen
again!
Lady S Excellent!

They turn to the audience with evil laughter

Mefisto And ... er ... the little matter of payment?
Lady S (*handing him one wad of notes*) This now! And the rest when
you have successfully carried out the deed.
Mefisto (*gloating over the money*) Ah! [Posh area], here I come! (*He
puts the money in his pocket*)
Lady S I want it done straight away. Immediately.
Mefisto I would suggest that it be done tonight, your ladyship. Under
cover of darkness. We don't want any witnesses.
Lady S Very well. I will leave the details to you. Just make sure that
Bo-Peep disappears *forever!*
Mefisto Oh, she will, your ladyship! (*To the audience*) Oh, yes, she
will!
Audience Oh, no, she won't!

Mefisto ⎫ (*together*) Oh, yes, she will!
Lady S ⎭

This continues ad-lib

Mefisto exits DR, *amid boos and hisses*

Lady S (*to the audience, with wicked glee*) And so, you puny peasants, my problem is solved. As from tonight, Bo-Peep will no longer stand between Freddie and I! He will be mine! All mine! Ha! Ha! Ha! And if *you* continue to displease me, I will get Mefisto to make *you* disappear as well! Ha! Ha! Ha!

Laughing, she exits DL

The Lights fade to Black-out

Music to cover the scene change

SCENE 5

The Village Green, that night

As Act I, Scene 1. Moonlight effect

The Villagers are discovered. They are singing and making merry outside the Inn. During this, Barmaids come from the inn and perform a dance routine

Song 8

The Villagers cheer and applaud the Barmaids

The Publican (Male or Female) enters from the inn

Publican (*calling*) Time, gentlemen, please!

Groans from the Villagers

Come along! Haven't you got any homes to go to?

The Villagers hastily drink up

The Barmaids collect their tankards and exit into the inn. A few more Villagers come out of the inn and join the others. They all drift out in various directions

(Calling into the inn) Come on, Fanny! I'm waiting to close up!

Fanny comes out of the inn

Fanny All right! All right! Don't get yer pinny in a pickle! Who do you think you are — [Publican from TV Soap]?

The Publican exits into the inn

Fanny spots the audience

Oh! Hello, folks! I bet you're surprised to see me coming out of this kind of hostility, aren't you? I usually frequent the [local "Posh" hotel]! You get a much better class of boozer in there. They always apologize when they sit on your Pork Scratchings. I'm only here to give Wally my mortal support. He's still determined to ask that Cindy Sparkle out. He's been in there to get a drop of Dutch courage.

Wally comes out of the inn. He is a little tipsy and unsteady on his feet

Here he comes! Look, Wally! Our mates are here.

Wally staggers upstage and waves at the backcloth

(Yelling to him) OY!! We're over here! *(To the audience)* He'll need Sat Nav for this!

Wally turns and makes his unsteady way downstage. He gives the Audience a lopsided grin

Wally 'Ello!
Audience Hello!
Wally *(peering at the Audience)* Tha's funny! There seems to be a lot more of 'em!
Fanny That's *you!* You're seeing double!
Wally A double! Good idea! *(He staggers to the inn)*
Fanny *(pulling him back)* I think it's time you went home. The pigs will be waitin' up for you.

Wally Oi don't care! Oi be gonna find Cindy! (*He sighs*) Oh! Cindy Sparkle! (*He leans against Fanny*) Did oi tell you oi *luuuv* Cindy Sparkle?

Fanny About a million times!

Wally Oi be gonna find 'er! Right now! (*He staggers away to* L) Who moved the door?

Fanny (*going after him*) It's too late. She'll be tucked up in bed with Stephen King.

Wally She'd better not be!

Fanny Let's go home. You can look for her in the morning.

Wally But oi wanna see her *now!* Oi be all fired up! (*He staggers and nearly falls over*)

Fanny I think your boiler's busted! Come on! (*She moves away to exit* R)

Wally 'Ere! (*He staggers over to her*) Oi see they'm back together again!

Fanny Who?

Wally The cheeks of yer bum! (*He guffaws*)

Fanny raises her fist, then changes her mind

Fanny (*to the audience*) There's no point hittin' him. In his present state he won't feel it!

The baa-ing of sheep is heard at the back

Wally (*to Fanny*) Wos that you?

The Sheep file on from the back. They are followed by Bo-Peep and Freddie

Wally Oh, look! It's Little Bo-Sheep and 'er Peep! (*Waving to sheep*) 'Ello, little sheepies!

Freddie (*smiling*) What's the matter with him?

Fanny He's had a sniff of the barmaid's apron! What are you doing here?

Bo-Peep It's time to settle the sheep down for the night.

Fanny (*to the sheep*) Oh! Is Mummy's little darlings tired den?

Sheep Baa! Baa!

Freddie (*to Bo-Peep*) Are you sure you want to stay with them all night, on your own?

Bo-Peep Perfectly sure. I've done it lots of times before. It's what I'm paid for, remember. To look after the sheep, by day *and* by night.

Wally Ar! You know the old song — (*Singing*) "While shepherds wash their socks by night, all seated on the ground ..."
Fanny Yes! That's enough of that! (*To Freddie*) Let Bo-Peep do her job, and help me take Aled Jones 'ere home.
Freddie (*to Bo-Peep*) Well ... if you're sure.
Bo-Peep Of course I'm sure.
Freddie Good-night then, Bo.
Bo-Peep Good-night, Freddie.

They go into a fond embrace

Wally (*emotionally overcome by the sight*) Oo! That's what oi'd like to do with Cindy! Oi'd like to cuddle 'er all up! (*He throws his arms around Fanny and cuddles her*)
Fanny (*disentangling herself*) Ger off! Come on, Freddie! Let's get him home before he makes an expedition of himself!

Wally starts singing again. Fanny and Freddie manoeuvre him out R

Bo-Peep (*to her flock*)   And now, my little sheep,
                                    Are you ready to go to sleep?
Sheep (*shaking their heads*) Baa! Baa!
Bo-Peep   Well, settle down and try,
                                    While I sing you this lullaby.

The music starts. The Sheep get into a huddle and lie down C. *Bo-Peep moves about, singing to them*

Song 9

It might be nice if the sheep could join in with bleated responses

By the end of the number, the Sheep have fallen asleep. On tiptoe, Bo-Peep moves to R, *and sits under a tree. After a while, her head begins to nod and she falls asleep herself*

Mefisto creeps on from L. *He sees Bo-Peep and gives an unpleasant laugh*

Mefisto   Ha! Ha! Ha!
                  There she is! Little Bo-Peep!
                  At my mercy and fast asleep! (*He raises his arms*)
                  I summon the powers of sorcery!
                  Come to my aid and work for me!

*There is a great crash of thunder. The lighting becomes dark and sinister.
Mefisto gives his demonic laugh. Amazingly, none of this wakes Bo-Peep
or the Sheep!*

> Ha! Ha! Ha! When she wakes, she will not be here!
> She will be in a place of dread and fear!
> All hopes of returning she can banish!
> Now to make her — completely *vanish!*

*He is about to make the magic pass at Bo-Peep, when Lady Sneering
suddenly enters from* L

Lady S Have you done it?

*This startles Mefisto and causes him to make the magic pass at the
Sheep, instead of at Bo-Peep!*

There is a flash, followed by a complete Black-out

The Sheep exit

*The Lights return to normal. The Sheep have vanished from the scene.
Mefisto and Lady Sneering gape at the empty space, and then at the still
sleeping Bo-Peep*

Lady S (*infuriated*) She's still here! What happened?
Mefisto (*flustered*) It ... It was your fault!
Lady S What!
Mefisto I was just about to cast the spell when you startled me! I made
the *sheep* disappear instead of *her!*
Lady S You idiot! You incompetent fool!
Mefisto (*protesting*) It was an accident!
Lady S *You're* the accident! Well, don't just stand there! Make Bo-Peep
disappear! *Now!*
Mefisto It will mean summoning the forces again.
Lady S I don't care if it means summoning the [topical/ local reference]!
Do it!
Mefisto Very well. (*He raises his arms*)
> I summon the powers of sorcery ...
Freddie (*off* R, *calling*) *Bo! Are you all right! Bo!*
Mefisto There's someone coming! Let's get away from here!

Mefisto runs out L. *Reluctantly, Lady Sneering follows him out*

Freddie rushes on from R

He goes to Bo-Peep, who is starting to wake up

Freddie Bo! ... Bo! ... Are you all right?
Bo-Peep Freddie? ... Why are you ... I must have fallen asleep ...
Freddie (*helping her up*) I heard some strange noises. I wondered if there was something wrong.
Bo-Peep Strange noises? I ... (*with sudden alarm*) The sheep! Are they all right? (*She looks to where the sheep should be and lets out a startled cry*)
Freddie What's wrong?
Bo-Peep The sheep! They aren't here! They're gone! Where are they? (*She searches about the stage in desperation*) *Where are they?!*
Freddie Calm down, Bo. They've probably just wandered off somewhere. (*Looking off stage*) They can't have gone far.
Bo-Peep But they were all asleep! Oh, where *are* they, Freddie? What's happened to them?

The Villagers rush on from various directions

Villagers What's the matter? What's going on? Is something wrong?
Bo-Peep My sheep have gone missing! Have you seen them?

The Villagers shake their heads

Fanny (*off* R, *calling*) Freddie! *Freddie!*

Fanny rushes on from R. *She now wears an outrageous nightdress, cap and curlers*

What's goin' on out 'ere? What's all the commotion about? I was just goin' to bed! (*Business with nightdress*) As you can see from my negligence!
Bo-Peep (*rushing to Fanny, in tears*) Oh! Mrs Fairacre!
Fanny (*comforting her*) Now, now! What's wrong, dear? (*To Freddie, sternly*) What have you been doing to her?
Freddie I'm afraid we've got some bad news, Mum. The sheep seem to have gone missing!
Fanny You *what?*
Bo-Peep (*tearfully*) They were asleep ... right here ... I must have dozed off ... when I woke up — *they'd gone!*
Fanny Where?

Bo-Peep I don't know! I don't know! Oh, I'm so sorry! (*She cries and buries her face in her hands*)
Fanny They must be around here somewhere! (*To the Villagers*) Don't just stand there, you lot! Help me find those sheep!

Fanny rushes out R, *calling*

(*Off*) Sheep! Where are yah? Come to Mummy! Sheeeep!

Dramatic music creeps in. The Villagers run out in various directions. Bo-Peep rushes into Freddie's arms

Bo-Peep Oh, Freddie! Where are they? *Where are they?*

Freddie tries to comfort her. Dramatic music up to full, as —

— *The* CURTAIN *falls*

ACT II

SCENE 1

Fanny's Farmyard

The back cloth shows countryside with the village in the distance. Across the back is a low fence with an opening in the centre. A farmhouse is R, *with practical door. There is a barn* L, *with practical door. Entrances at the back and* R *and* L

The Chorus and Dancers, as Farmhands, are discovered. They go straight into a lively song and dance

Song 10

After the number, Fanny comes out of the farmhouse. She is not in a good mood

Fanny Don't know what you lot have got to sing and dance about.
Farmhands Good-morning, Mrs Fairacre!
Fanny What's *good* about it? Have you found my sheep?
Farmhands No.
Fanny I thought not!
1st Farmhand Wull, we were up *all* last night lookin' for 'em.
Farmhands Ar!
Fanny That shouldn't stop you looking for 'em now! Go on! Get lookin'!

The Farmhands, rather reluctantly, exit in various directions

(*To the audience, gloomily*) Hello folks. Sorry I'm not me usual sunny self, but I'm so worried about the missing sheep. Poor things. What could have happened to them. Hey! You don't think they've been via-ducted by aliens, do yah?
Audience No!
Fanny No, that's silly, isn't it. I bet somebody nicked 'em! I wouldn't put it past some around 'ere! They'd steal your teeth if they weren't nailed down. Yes, that's got to be it. I mean, they didn't just disappear as if by magic, did they?

Audience Yes!

Fanny What? You think they *did?* You think they disappeared by magic?

Audience Yes!

Fanny (*scoffing*) Oh, come on! *Now* who's being silly?

Freddie and Bo-Peep enter L. *Bo-Peep is looking very upset and tearful*

Freddie Hello, Mum.

Fanny Any luck, Freddie?

Freddie (*sadly*) No, I'm sorry. There's not a sign of them anywhere. We even went all the way to [Local place].

Fanny Well, even lost sheep wouldn't go *there!* But thanks for trying.

Bo-Peep (*weepily*) I'm sorry! This is all my fault. It was my responsibly to look after them, and I've let you down. Can you ever forgive me?

Fanny Well, by rights I ought to give you the sack! But I'm not going to. You'd probably sue me for unfair epistle, or something like that. Besides, I reckon somebody stole 'em.

Freddie (*smiling in spite of himself*) Sheep rustlers? Surely not.

Fanny Well, if you think that's daft, you want to hear what our friends think. *They* think the sheep disappeared by magic! Potty, isn't it? They've been watching too much *Doctor Who!* No. Somebody nicked 'em! And if they don't show up today, I'll have to report it to the police.

Bo-Peep (*bursting into tears*) Oh! I'm sorry! I'm so sorry!

Fanny Take her into the house and make her a nice cup o' tea, Freddie. And as she's been to [Local place mentioned earlier], you'd better put a drop of something in it.

Freddie and Bo-Peep exit into the farmhouse

(*To the audience*) Oh, well! Life goes on. I've still got all the other animals to tend to. And talking of dumb creatures, I haven't seen that useless Wally this morning.

Wally is heard groaning loudly off stage at the back

Crikey! (*To the audience*) Was that you? It's not that bad, is it?

Groaning, Wally enters at the back. He is suffering from a hangover and is holding his head and stomach

Wally (*groaning*) Oooh! Me head! Oooh! Me stomach! (*He staggers downstage*)
Fanny Here he is! The living dead!
Wally Oooh! Never again! Never again!
Fanny (*going right up to him and bellowing in his ear*) Mornin'!!
Wally (*flinching with pain*) Aaagh! (*Peering at her*) Oh, 'tis you, missus. If you're gonna speak, d'you mind doin' it from right over there. (*He moves away, holding his head*) Oooh! Me achin' head!

Fanny has a mischievous idea. She goes upstage and picks up a metal bucket and ladle. Winking to the audience, she creeps up behind Wally, and bangs the ladle against the bucket. Wally nearly jumps out of his skin and covers his ears

Wally (*in agony*) Oooh! Don't *do* that!
Fanny (*stopping*) What?... *This!* (*She bangs the bucket again*)

She chases Wally around the stage, making the awful racket. He eventually falls to his knees, begging for mercy. Fanny stops making the racket

Fanny (*standing right over him*) Got a huge hangover, have yah? Serve you right.
Wally You can talk! (*Indicating her chest*) You've got a *huge hangover* as well. (*He guffaws, but it hurts!*)
Fanny (*threatening him with the bucket and ladle*) D'you want some more of this?
Wally (*flinching away*) Oi'm sorry! Oi'm sorry!
Fanny I hope you've learnt your lesson. That's what you get for thinking you had a chance with that Cindy Sparkle.
Wally (*getting to his feet*) Oi still do! Oi be goin' to see her. Just as soon as me head clears.
Fanny Well, that shouldn't take long! It's empty already! Anyway, *you're* not going anywhere. We're short handed this morning. They're all out looking for the missing sheep. That means you and me'll have to milk Buttercup, the cow.
Wally (*protesting*) But oi be a *pig* boy not a cowboy!
Fanny You'll be a *flat* boy in a minute! Go and fetch Buttercup!

Wally slouches out L

Fanny puts away the bucket and ladle

Wally (*off* L, *calling*) Whoa! Buttercup! Whoa!

Buttercup, the cow, canters on from L. *She trots around the stage, with Wally holding on to her tail*

Suitable music plays as Buttercup enters. Eventually, Wally and Fanny get Buttercup under control and lead her DS

Fanny Now then, Buttercup, are you going to be a good girl for Mummy?
Buttercup (*mooing and nodding her head*) Mooo!
Fanny That's right. There's some nice people I'd like you to meet. Look, here they are. (*She indicates the audience*)

Buttercup looks at them

Would you like to say hello?

Buttercup shakes her head

Why not?

Buttercup whispers in her ear

(*To the audience*) She says she's shy. Ahh!

Shyly, Buttercup turns her back on the audience

Wally (*to the audience*) That's what she thinks of you!
Fanny (*to the audience*) Tell you what, folks. If you call out "Hello, Buttercup", she'll know there's nothing to be shy about. Let's give it a try.
Audience Hello, Buttercup!

Buttercup doesn't move

Wally (*to the audience*) Try again. A bit louder this time.
Audience Hello, Buttercup!

Buttercup part turns

Fanny Nearly. Once more.
Audience Hello, Buttercup!

Buttercup turns to face the audience

Fanny That's it! (*To Buttercup*) See. There's nothing to be shy about, is there?

Buttercup shakes her head

Now you can say hello to them.
Buttercup (*to the audience*) Moo! Moo!
Fanny (*to the audience*) She's a very intelligent cow, isn't she, boys and girls?
Audience Yes!
Wally Ar! She's always reading the paper.
Fanny What paper?
Wally The *Moos* of the World! (*He guffaws*)

Buttercup kicks him with her back leg

Fanny (*patting the cow*) Well done, Buttercup! Now it's time for *you-know-what!*

Buttercup reacts and backs away

Oh, come on, there's a good girl. You know you've got to be milked.

Buttercup shakes her head

Yes, you have. I promise I'll warm my hands. (*To Wally*) You keep hold of her while I fetch the stool.

Wally holds Buttercup, while Fanny collects the stool, positions and sits on it

(*Tapping her lap*) Come on! Come to mummy! Come on!

Wally backs Buttercup over to Fanny. The back half of the cow sits down on Fanny's lap

(*Yelling*) Ahhhgh! Get her off! Get her off!

Wally leads Buttercup away. Fanny gets up and does a comically painful walk up and down

(*To the Audience*) Cor! That brought tears to me eyes! (*To Wally*) Let's do it properly this time! (*She sits on the stool again*)

Wally positions Buttercup so that her head is facing Fanny

How long do you think my arms are?! The other way round, you clot!

Wally turns Buttercup around and positions her correctly

The bucket! Fetch the bucket!

Wally collects a plastic bucket and puts it down. Buttercup kicks it away

Wally Cor! The [local football team] could do with you, Buttercup!

Wally retrieves the bucket and put it in the right place. Fanny flexes her fingers and starts milking

Fanny Is anything coming out?
Wally (*bending down to look*) Nope! (*To the Audience*) It must be evaporated milk!
Fanny Oh, dear! I'll have to try a different method.

She stands up, takes hold of Buttercup's tail and uses it like a pump. After a while, a plastic bottle of milk drops into the bucket. With a cheer, Wally holds it up to show the audience. Fanny keeps pumping. A packet of butter drops into the bucket. With another cheer, Wally holds it up to the audience. Fanny is getting very weary

Wally Don't stop now, missus! Go for the big one!

Fanny keeps pumping. A box of chocolates drops into the bucket. Wally cheers and holds them up to the audience

A box of milk chocolates!

Fanny stops pumping and collapses against Buttercup's rear

(*Making a fuss of the cow*) Well done, Buttercup! Who's a clever old cow, then?
Fanny Oy! What about *me?!*
Wally Oh, you're a clever old cow too! (*He guffaws*)
Fanny (*to the audience*) I think she deserves a round of claps for that.

The Audience applauds. Buttercup bows and curtsies to them. Fanny leads Buttercup forward. Wally picks up the stool and the bucket. He puts the milk, butter and chocolates in it

Fanny (*to Buttercup*) I expect you're feeling tired after all that. I know I am.
Buttercup (*wilting against her*) Moooo!
Fanny I thought so. Wally'll take you back to your field and you can have a nice lie down.
Wally (*moving down and taking charge of Buttercup*) Ar! Come on, old girl. Say goodbye to the nice people before you go.
Buttercup (*to the audience*) Moo! Moo!
Fanny Goodbye, Buttercup!

Wally leads Buttercup towards exit L

Oy! Not so fast! (*She crosses to Wally and takes the box of chocolates out of the bucket*) Them's mine!
Wally Oi thought you were tryin' to diet!
Fanny Wrong! I'm dyin' to try it!

Wally exits with Buttercup L

Fanny (*to the audience*) I shall enjoy these. You don't want any, do you? Oh, you do! All right. I'll save you the ones with the hard centres. I always spit them out!

Fanny goes into the house

Lady Sneering and Mefisto creep on at the back. They look about, and then make their way down stage

Lady S This is the farm where Bo-Peep works. Ugh! What a *revolting* smell!
Mefisto That's not coming from the farm, your ladyship. It's coming from *them!* (*He indicates the audience*)
Lady S (*sneering at the audience*) Yes, you're right! Those *smelly* commoners are still here! (*To the audience*) Why don't you go away, and take your nasty smells with you!
Mefisto (*to the audience*) Yes! And your nasty little faces! (*By-play with the audience*)
Lady S Enough of this! You have work to do, Mefisto. You must rectify your abysmal mistake from last night.
Mefisto That was really your fault, your ladyship: if you hadn't —
Lady S Silence! You want the rest of the money, don't you?
Mefisto (*slavering*) Oh, yes, your ladyship!
Lady S Then you must do the thing properly this morning! You must make sure that Bo-Peep disappears *forever!*

Mefisto I will, your ladyship.
Lady S Then delay no longer. She must be here somewhere. (*Moving to the farmhouse*) I will enquire at this rustic ruin.
Mefisto (*rushing to Lady Sneering*) Wait, your ladyship! She needs to be on her own. No witnesses, remember.
Lady S (*grudgingly*) Oh, very well. Conceal yourself, and I will make sure that she is quite alone.

Mefisto looks about, and then creeps into the barn L

Lady Sneering knocks on the farmhouse door

Freddie opens it and comes out

Freddie Oh! Good-morning, your ladyship.
Lady S (*aside*) Oh! He looks handsomer than ever! (*To Freddie*) Good-morning, Freddie.
Freddie Can I help you?
Lady S (*aside*) Oh! In so many, many ways! (*To him*) I was wondering if ...

Bo-Peep comes out of the house

Bo-Peep (*with a nice curtsy*) Good-morning, your ladyship.
Lady S (*to the audience*) Bah! How I *loathe* the very sight of her! (*To Freddie, completely ignoring Bo-Peep*) I am thinking of purchasing a new horse for my stables. Have you any for sale?
Freddie Yes, several. What sort of horse had you in mind?
Lady S Oh, the usual sort. One with four legs and a tail. (*She goes to Freddie, and taking his arm, drawing him away from Bo-Peep*) Perhaps if you were to show me what you have on offer, I could choose one that takes my fancy.
Freddie Certainly, your ladyship. This way.

They move towards exit L. *Freddie turns*

Would you like to come with us, Bo?
Bo-Peep (*about to follow*) All right.
Lady S (*firmly*) *NO!* That will *not* be necessary!

Lady Sneering practically hauls Freddie out L

Bo-Peep (*to the audience, moving* DS) What a strange woman Lady Sneering is. It's almost as if she resented my being with Freddie. I wonder why? (*She moves to exit* L, *and looks off*)

Mefisto creeps from the barn

Mefisto   Bo-Peep alone! There is no one here!
                   Now to make her disappear! (*He raises his arms*)
                   I summon the powers of sorcery!
                   Come to my aid and work for me!

*There is a great crash of thunder. The lighting becomes dark and sinister.
Bo-Peep reacts with terror. Mefisto creeps up behind her. The audience
will be shouting out warnings*

Bo-Peep (*to the audience*) What's wrong? What's happening?
Audience He's behind you!

Mefisto is about to cast the spell on Bo-Peep

Suddenly Buttercup trots on from R

The lighting returns to normal

Wally (*off* R, *yelling*) Buttercup! Come back 'ere!
Mefisto (*to the audience*) Curses! Foiled again!

Mefisto runs out L

Wally runs on from R. *He chases Buttercup around the stage. He tries
to grab her tail, but falls over*

Mooing triumphantly, Buttercup escapes at the back

Fanny comes out of the farmhouse

Fanny What's all the noise about? (*Seeing Wally on the ground*) Oh, no!
   (*She hauls him up by his collar*) Have you been at the special brew again?
Wally It was Buttercup! She gave oi the slip!
Fanny And I'm sure you'll look lovely in it. (*Seeing Bo-Peep and
   moving to her*) What's the matter, Bo-Peep? You seem a bit flustered.
Bo-Peep (*putting her hand to her head, confused*) I ... I don't know ...
   there was something ...

Freddie and Lady Sneering enter from L. *Seeing that Bo-Peep is still very
much in evidence, Lady Sneering lets out a frustrated and angry cry*

Lady S *Ahhhhhhgh!!*

Fanny (*reacting*) Crikey! Are you in pain?
Lady S No! (*Venomously*) But I know someone who very soon *will be!*

With an angry growl, Lady Sneering storms out L

Fanny (*to the audience*) Nice woman! A friend of yours?
Freddie Are you all right, Bo? (*Going to her*) You look troubled.
Fanny Oh, she's worried about the lost sheep. We all are. We need something to cheer us up.
Wally Shall oi tell one of my jokes?
Fanny I said *cheer* up, not *throw* up!
Wally How about a song!
Fanny Good idea! (*To the audience*) You knew that was comin', didn't yah? (*To the Conductor/Pianist*) Take it away, Elton!

Song 11

Song and dance

The Farmhands enter and join in

Perhaps Buttercup can trot on and participate

The number ends and the Lights fade to Black-out. Music to cover the scene change

SCENE 2

Near the farm

Tabs, or the front cloth used in Act I, Scene 2

Ding and Dong enter from DR. *They greet the audience*

Duo Hello, folks! Hi, kids!
Dong I bet they've forgotten all about us.
Ding No one could forget a face like yours!
Dong What's wrong with it? I've got a very sweet face.
Ding Yes. It looks like it's made of sugar.
Dong (*very pleased*) Thanks.
Ding And somebody's licked it!
Dong Well, you can't have brains *and* beauty.

Ding Oh, you've got brains, have you?

Dong Yeah! My head's just *bursting* with 'em!

Ding Is that what it is! I thought you just needed a hair cut. All right, brainy. Do you know the difference between a letter box and an elephant's bum?

Ding No.

Dong Then I won't be asking *you* to post any letters! What do you call a boomerang that doesn't come back?

Dong Pass.

Ding A stick! (*À la Anne Robinson*) Dong! You *are* the weakest link. Goodbye!

Dong hangs his head, and does "The Walk of Shame" off DR

(*To the audience, sighing*) Ahh! Shall I get him back?

Audience Yes!

Ding goes off DR, *and returns with a downcast Dong*

Ding (*putting his arm around him*) Cheer up. You might not be an Egghead, but I'm still your mate.

Dong (*cheering up*) Yeah! And with friends like you, who needs enemas!

Song 12

Comedy "Friendship" song for Ding and Dong

After the number, Wally enters from DR. *He is wearing his "best". This consists of a loud check suit that is far too small, and a hat that is far too big. He also wears a wide gaudy tie and has an enormous flower in his button hole*

Ding Look! It's [current personality to suit]!

Wally Marnin'!

Duo (*copying his accent*) Marnin'!

Wally (*moving to them*) 'Ere! You two work for Cindy Sparkle, don't 'ee?

Duo Oh, ar!

Wally Be she *seein'* anyone?

Dong Only when she's got her eyes open.

Wally What oi mean is ... does she 'ave a *current* boyfriend?

Dong No, but she's got a *BlackBerry* phone!

Ding Why do *you* want to know?

Wally (*proudly*) 'Cos oi be gonna ask 'er out! Thas why oi be all dressed up like this!

Ding Oh! We thought you were auditioning for the circus! (*Or something current to suit*)

Wally Oi've got to give a good impression.

Dong You have! (*Pointing to the flower*) Of a grow-bag!

Wally Oi've had a bath, a shower and oi've been through the sheep dip twice.

Ding Did you wash behind your ears?

Wally Ar! All three of 'em.

Dong *Three* of them?!

Wally Ar! (*Pointing to various parts of his anatomy*) 'Ere! 'Ere! An' 'ere! Oi've sprayed meself all over! (*Lifting up his arms*) Smell!

They do so, and reel away, coughing and sputtering

That's Lynx!

Ding Did he say Lynx, or *stinks?!*

Wally Can you smell my aftershave? (*He wafts it towards them*)

Dong Smell it! It's burnt the hairs up my nose!

Wally (*preening himself*) Oi reckon oi look a million dollars.

Ding More like a crumpled ten pound note!

Wally Cindy Sparkle's bound to wanna go out with oi. (*To someone in the audience*) Oi bet *you'd* go out wi' oi, wouldn't ee? No, not you, *zur!* Oi was talkin' to that young lady. (*By-play with the audience, then to Ding and Dong*) Well, Oi'm off!

Ding
Dong } (*together*) You can say that again!

Wally (*psyching himself up*) Cindy Sparkle, 'ere oi come! (*To the audience*) Wish oi luck, folks!

Audience Good luck!

Wally adjusts his hat and marches confidently to the exit DL. Once there, his courage fails him and he timidly sneaks out

Ding and Dong have a good laugh

Dong D'you think Cindy *will* go out with him?

Ding You never know. Strange things can happen.

Dong That's true. Look at [topical or local gag]!

Ding (*looking off* DR) Oh, no! Look who's coming this way!

Dong (*looking*) It's murky Mefisto!

Ding And he's got that snooty Lady Sneering with him.

Dong Cor! She's giving him a right ear bashin' by the look of it.

Ding I wonder what she's saying to him. Let's hide and find out.
Dong Yeah! Let's do some ears drooping!
Ding *Eavesdropping!*
Dong Is she! Where?

Ding pushes Dong out DL, *where they hide with just their heads poking
out*

Mefisto enters DR, *followed by an enraged Lady Sneering*

Lady S You incompetent fool! That's twice you have failed to rid me of
Bo-Peep! What happened this time, you bungler?
Mefisto Cow!
Lady S (*outraged*) *What* did you call me?!
Mefisto Not you, your ladyship. This was the *four* legged variety. It
came along just as I was about to cast the spell on the girl.
Lady S (*sarcastically*) Ha! It's a wonder you didn't make it disappear
like you did those sheep!
Mefisto There was someone with the animal. I couldn't risk being
seen.
Lady S A fine magician, you are! I have a good mind to take my money
back.
Mefisto You can't. I've already used it to buy a house in [local "posh"
area]. And I need the rest of the money to buy furniture at [local store]!
Please give me another chance, your ladyship.
Lady S Very well. But if you fail me a third time, you will have to get
your furniture from [local refuge tip]!
Mefisto (*grovelling*) Thank you, your ladyship, thank you.
Lady S Then stop wasting time. Let us find Bo-Peep! And dispose of
her — *once and for all!*

Laughing their evil laughs, they exit DR

Ding and Dong emerge from hiding

Ding Cor! What a dastardly duo!
Dong Yeah! They're a right pair of dastards!
Ding So! Mefisto was responsible for the missing sheep. He made them
disappear!
Dong And now he's gonna do the same to poor Bo-Peep. We can't let
that happen, can we?
Ding No! Let's run and tell Cindy. She'll know what to do.
Dong Right! Come on, Batman! There's not a moment to lose!

In their haste, they crash into each other, and then run out DL, *as the Lights fade to Black-out*

Music to cover the scene change, and then the Lights come up on —

SCENE 3

In the show tent

As Act I, Scene 3

Cindy and the troupe of Dancers are discovered. All are wearing clown costumes and masks. They go straight into a song and dance routine

Song 13

After the number, the Dancers relax and get their breath back

Cindy (*pushing her mask up*) That was fine, girls. But it still needs a bit of work. Take a ten minute break, and we'll do the whole routine again.

The Dancers exit L

Cindy replaces her mask and does a few exercises. She touches her toes

Wally enters nervously from R. *He sees Cindy, and moves timidly down to her*

Wally (*addressing her rear end*) Er ... Excuse oi ...

Cindy straightens up and turns to face him. He reacts at the sight of the clown mask

Waa! ... Hello! Oi be looking for Cindy Sparkle. Be she 'ere?

Cindy just nods

Good ... Do you know her very well?

Cindy nods

Oi ... oi hear she ain't got a boyfriend.

Cindy shakes her head

Do you ... do you reckon she'd go out with oi? 'Cos tha's why oi be
'ere ... to ask her out. Oi be proper nervous. Oi know she's tons better
than oi. Oi be only a poor, scruffy pig boy, and she be a beautiful
dancer an' all ... But ... you see ... Oi fell in love with 'er the moment oi
set eyes on 'er. (*Rapturously*) Oh! Oi be head over heels in love with
Cindy Sparkle, oi be! (*Then sighing, sadly*) But oi reckon oi were daft
comin' 'ere. She wouldn't be interested in the likes of oi. Oi'd better
go afore oi makes a fool of meself. (*He moves towards the exit* R)

*Cindy goes after him and touches his arm. He stops and turns. Cindy
pushes up her clown mask. Wally is staggered, to say the least!*

Waa! It's woo ... Oi mean, *you!* ... Oi mean ... *Oh, 'elp!* (*He makes a
dash for the exit*)
Cindy (*stopping him*) Wait! Don't go. I don't even know your name.
What is it?
Wally (*a gibbering wreck*) It's ... It's ... Oh, oi forgot! (*To the audience,
desperate*) What's my name?!
Audience Wally!
Wally Ar! Tha's right! ... Wally! (*To Cindy*) Oi be Wally. (*Miserably*)
A *right* wally!
Cindy Did you really mean what you said?
Wally W ... What did oi said?
Cindy That you fell in love with me the moment you saw me.
Wally (*in torment*) D ... Did oi s ... s ... say that?
Cindy Yes. And you also said (*She mimics him, but not unkindly*) "Oi
be head over heels in love with Cindy Sparkle, oi be!"
Wally Oi ... Oi were talkin' about somebody else!
Cindy (*smiling*) I don't think there can be *two* people called Cindy
Sparkle.
Wally (*in complete misery*) Ooooh!
Cindy (*taking his arm and leading him* DS) I don't mind at all. I'm really
very flattered.
Wally Oi shouldn't 'ave said those things. Oi didn't know it were you.
Oi thought you were just a clown. Now *oi* be the clown.
Cindy I don't think you're a clown at all, Wally. (*Taking his hands*) I
think you're very nice.
Wally (*surprised*) Oh! (*To the audience*) Ooooh!
Cindy Well, here I am! You came to ask me out, didn't you?
Wally Ar!
Cindy Well, go on. Ask me.

Wally (*taking a big breath, and then gabbling it out*) Will you go out with oi? (*He cringes, expecting the worst*)
Cindy Yes.
Wally Eh?
Cindy Yes. I will go out with you, Wally.
Wally (*elated*) You will! (*To the audience, elated*) Cor! She said yes, folks!
Cindy Where are you going to take me?
Wally To the moon! To the moon! (*Coming down to earth*) But first you'll have to settle for the [local pub]!

Song 14

Comedy "romantic" duet for Wally and Cindy

At the end of the number, Wally bashfully kisses Cindy on the cheek. He then presents his cheek to be kissed. Cindy grabs him, and bends him over in a very "passionate" kiss

At this point, Ding and Dong rush on from R

Ding (*putting his hand over Dong's eyes*) Don't look! You're too young!
Dong (*pushing his hand away*) What's that clown doing to him?
Ding That clown is Cindy!
Dong Oh! D'you think he's asking her out?
Ding I think they've reached the next level. (*He taps Cindy on the shoulder*) Excuse me.

Wally and Cindy come out of the embrace. Wally is blissfully breathless!

Wally (*gasping*) She said yes!
Ding I hate to interrupt this scene from *Hollyoaks*, but something terrible is going to happen.
Cindy What's wrong?
Dong It's Mefisto! He's gonna make Little Bo-Peep disappear!
Cindy Why?
Dong We don't know. But that snooty Lady Sneering's got something to do with it. We overheard 'em talking.
Ding She's paying Mefisto to get rid of Bo-Peep. He tried to do it before, but only managed to make her sheep disappear.
Dong We've got to stop him. We thought you might know how, Cindy.

Cindy I'll help, of course. The question is — *how?* As you know, Mefisto is no ordinary magician. He has command of dark and evil forces. The only way to fight magic is *with* magic. If only ... Where is he now?

Ding Out searching for Bo-Peep.

Cindy I'll look in his caravan. He has lots of books dealing with the black arts, witchcraft, magic spells and that sort of thing. I might be able to find something that will help us.

Ding How do you know what to look for?

Cindy I don't. But it's all I can think of. It's worth a try. In the meantime, you two go and find Bo-Peep before Mefisto does. Hide her somewhere where he can't find her.

Ding }
Dong } *(together)* Right!

Ding and Dong run out R

Wally What shall *oi* do — *beloved?*

Cindy You wait here and keep a lookout for Mefisto.

Wally But what about our date?

Cindy At the moment I think it's more important to help Bo-Peep, don't you?

Wally *(pouting)* Oi suppose so.

Cindy Don't worry. There'll be plenty of time for us later.

Wally *(bashfully)* Can oi ... Can oi 'ave something to be goin' on with?

As before, Cindy bends him over in a "passionate" kiss

Cindy lets him go, and runs out L

Overwhelmed, Wally almost slides to the ground

(To the audience) Corrr! Oi still *can't* believe it, folks. Cindy Sparkle be actually goin' out wi' oi!

Mefisto and Lady Sneering enter from R. *They creep up behind Wally*

The audience will be shouting warnings

Wally *(to the audience)* Eh? What's up? Is it Mefisto?

Audience Yes!

Wally *(nervously)* W ... Where is he?

Audience Behind you!

Comic business with Wally turning around slowly with the others keeping behind him. This can be repeated as desired. Eventually, Wally faces front again. Mefisto moves to one side of him and Lady Sneering to the other. Wally turns and comes face to face with Lady Sneering. He reacts, and then giggles

Wally (*to Lady Sneering*) *You're* not Mefisto! (*He turns to Mefisto, absently*) That lot said it was *you* ... (*He does a huge double take and lets out a yell*) Ahhgh! (*He tries to make a dash for it*)

Mefisto and Lady Sneering grab him and hold him firmly between them

Mefisto We are looking for Bo-Peep!
Wally Well, oi bain't 'er! In case you hadn't noticed, oi be of the male agenda!
Lady S Where is she? Where is Bo-Peep? *Tell us!* (*She twists his arm*)
Wally (*squirming*) Aooow! That 'urts!
Mefisto We will hurt you even more if you don't tell us where she is!
Lady S Yes! (*She twists his arm again*) *Tell us!* Where is Bo-Peep?
Mefisto Where is she?
Wally Oi don't know! Even if I did, oi wouldn't tell *you!* Oi know what you're gonna do to her! You're gonna make 'er disappear! Like you did the sheep!

Mefisto and Lady Sneering react and release Wally

Mefisto Curses! He knows!
Lady S Yes! He must be silenced! Dispose of him!
Mefisto With pleasure!
Wally (*quacking*) Oh, no! Oi'm too young and beautiful to die!
Mefisto Oh, you're not going to die.
Wally (*relaxing*) That's all right then.
Mefisto No, you are going to — *disappear!* You will never be seen again! Ha! Ha! Ha!
Wally (*wailing*) Ooooh!!
Mefisto (*with evil relish*) You will be sent to a place from which there is no return!
Wally Ooooh!
Mefisto A place that is worse than your worst nightmare!
Wally Ooooh!
Mefisto A place that ——
Lady S (*impatiently*) Stop wasting time! Get rid of him!
Mefisto (*miffed*) Oh! You take all the fun out of it.

Lady S *Do it!*
Mefisto Very well! (*He raises his arms*)
                  I summon the powers of sorcery!
                  Come to my aid and work for me!

*There is a great crash of thunder. The stage grows dark and sinister.
Wally shakes with fear*

                  I command you, dark forces that inhabit the night,
                  Remove this cretin, and take him from our sight!

There is a flash, followed by a complete Black-out

    Wally exits

*Mefisto's laughter is heard. The Lights return to normal. Wally has
vanished from the scene*

Lady S (*to Mefisto, sarcastically*) Well done! You got it right *this* time!
    (*To the audience, with evil relish*) And now to do the same with Little
    Bo-Peep! Come on! Ha! Ha! Ha!

Laughing their evil laughs, they exit R

Cindy enters on from L

Cindy (*as she enters*) It's no use! All his books are locked away, and ...
    Wally? (*She looks about; calling*) Wally? ... Where are you? ... Wally?
    (*To the audience*) Where is he? Where did he go?
Audience He disappeared! (*Etc.*)
Cindy Disappeared? Was it Mefisto? Did he make Wally disappear?
Audience Yes!
Cindy Oh, no! And we've only just met! Where is Mefisto now? Is he
    still looking for Bo-Peep?
Audience Yes!
Cindy I'd better try and find her before it's too late!

    Cindy runs out R

The Lights fade to Black-out

Dramatic music to cover the scene change

SCENE 4

Near the farm

As Act I, Scene 2

Bo-Peep and Freddie enter from DR

Freddie It's time to give up, Bo. We're not going to find the sheep. We've searched everywhere.
Bo-Peep (*sighing*) I know. I'm beginning to think our friends out there are right. They must have disappeared by magic.
Freddie (*laughing*) Surely you don't believe that.
Bo-Peep Well, what other explanation is there?
Freddie The one Mum gave. The sheep must have been stolen.
Bo-Peep Oh, it's all my fault. How could I let myself fall asleep like that?
Freddie (*smiling, and taking her hands*) I expect you were hoping to dream about me.

Song 15

Romanic duet with romantic lighting. After the number, the lighting returns to normal

Fanny enters from DR

Fanny (*greeting the audience*) Hello, folks! (*Seeing the embracing couple*) Oh! I see [current couple in the news] are at it again! (*Going to them*) Oy! Stop that! I've sent for the police.
Freddie About *us*?
Fanny No, you silly so-an'-so! About the stolen sheep. They're sending one of their finest officers. (*To the audience, excited*) I wonder who it'll be, folks? You never know, we might get Lewis, or Frost, or even [someone from a current TV police series]

PC Wurld enters from DL. *He is a typical example of the old-fashioned plodding village bobby. Helmet and big boots*

(*To the audience, deflated*) Or perhaps not!
PC Wurld 'Evenin' all. (*He bends his knees*) I'm PC Wurld. I'm looking for a Mrs Fanny Fairacre of Fairacre Farm.
Fanny (*going to him*) That's me!

PC Wurld I understand you've got a complaint. (*He bends his knees*)
Fanny And I'm not the only one by the look of it!
PC Wurld Beg your pardon?
Fanny Nothing! Yes. My sheep have been stolen!
PC Wurld Sheep, eh? (*He takes out a notebook and pencil*) When was this?
Freddie I think you'd better talk to Miss Bo-Peep, officer. She was there when the sheep went missing.
Bo-Peep Last night I was looking after the sheep, and I fell asleep. When I woke up they'd gone.
PC Wurld Where?
Fanny Somebody nicked 'em! It's obvious!
PC Wurld Not to me, it isn't.
Fanny No ... well ... Couldn't they have sent somebody else? Where's Inspector Barnaby? He'd have it all sorted out in two hours — *with adverts!*
PC Wurld I hope you're not being obstructive, madam.
Freddie It's quite simple. The sheep went missing. We've searched everywhere and can't find them. So, we've come to the conclusion that someone must have ...
Fanny *Nicked 'em!*
PC Wurld I see. Can you give me a description?
Fanny What of?
PC Wurld The sheep!
Fanny Crikey! You know what sheep look like, don't yah? They've got four legs with woolly bits in between.
PC Wurld (*writing laboriously in his notebook*) Four ... legs ... with ... woolly ... bits ... in ... between.
Fanny (*to the audience*) This is not so much *CSI*, as MFI!

A Farmhand rushes on from DR

Farmhand Missus! You'd better come! The pigs have got out! And we can't find 'em!
Fanny *What!* Where's Wally?
Farmhand Oi dunno! You'd better come quick!

Farmhand runs out DR

Fanny Oh, no! Not missing pigs as well!
Freddie I'll see to it, Mum!

Freddie runs out DR

PC Wurld Missing pigs, eh? I'd better go and investigate this! (*He crosses to exit* DR)

Fanny (*sarcastically*) D'you want a description? Four legs with curly tails!

PC Wurld gives her a look, bends his knees, and exits DR

Ding and Dong run on from DL

Ding Oh, Bo-Peep! Thank goodness we've found you in time!

Dong Yeah! Before *he* does!

Bo-Peep Who? What's going on?

Ding It's Mefisto! He's after you! He wants to make you disappear! Like he did in the show!

Dong Only this time he wants to make it peppermint — I mean — permanent!

Bo-Peep (*dumbfounded*) But why would he want to do that?

Ding We're not sure. That Lady Sneering's got something to do with it.

Dong He was the one who made your sheep disappear!

Fanny What! So, it was *him*! (*To the audience*) You were right, folks! It *was* magic, after all! Oh, that dirty, low down ... The police are here! I'll have him run in for this! (*Calling to off* DR) *Officer!*

Ding There's no time for that! Bo-Peep, you've got to hide from him! It's the only way!

Fanny He's right! We'll hide you somewhere on the farm! *Come on!*

They all rush to exit DR

Mefisto suddenly enters there

They all yell and rush to exit DL

Lady Sneering suddenly enters there

Lady Sneering and Mefisto laugh. The others retreat to C, *and huddle together in a terrified group*

Lady S (*to Mefisto*) There she is! Bo-Peep! What are you waiting for? Make her disappear at once!

Fanny You leave her alone! (*She hugs Bo-Peep, protectively*)

Duo (*doing the same*) Yeah!

Lady S (*to Mefisto*) Do it!

Mefisto But she's not alone!

Lady S Who cares! (*With evil relish*) Make them *all* disappear!
Mefisto Very well. (*He raises his arms*)
                    I summon the powers of sorcery!
                    Come to my aid and work for me!

There is a crash of thunder. The lighting becomes dark and sinister

                    I command you, dark forces that inhabit the night,
                    Remove these four persons from our sight!

There is a flash, followed by a complete Black-out

Fanny, Bo-Peep, Ding and Dong exit

When the Lights return to normal, there is an empty space C

Lady S Ha! Ha! Ha! (*To the audience, with evil glee*) Little Bo-Peep
is gone forever! No longer will she stand in my way! Now Freddie
Fairacre will be mine! *All mine!* Ha! Ha! Ha!
Mefisto (*moving to her*) I trust you are satisfied, your ladyship?
Lady S Oh, yes!
Mefisto And the money?
Lady S Here! (*She takes a wad of notes from her bag and gives it to
him*)
Mefisto (*drooling over it*) Thank you, your ladyship, thank you!
Lady S (*to audience*) Now to find the fabulous Freddie! It will give me
great pleasure telling him that Bo-Peep has decided to go away, never
to return! How sad the poor boy will be. But I will be there to comfort
him. Oh, yes! I will be ready with a very sympathetic shoulder for him
to cry on! With my irresistible charms, I will soon make him forget all
about that stupid Little Bo-Peep! Ha! Ha! Ha!

Laughing her sneering laugh, she exits DL

Mefisto (*gloating over the money*) Ha! Ha! Ha! [Furniture store] here
I come!

Cindy enters from DL. *At the same time, Freddie and PC Wurld enter
from* DR

Freddie (*as they enter*) We've found the pigs. They were ...
Cindy Ah, good! The police are here! (*Crossing to them and pointing
to Mefisto*) Officer! Arrest that magician!

PC Wurld Eh? ... Arrest ... (*Fumbling for his notebook*) On what charge?

Cindy He's planning to make Bo-Peep disappear!

Freddie } (*aghast*) *What!*
PC Wurld

Cindy In the same way he made her sheep disappear! *And* Wally!

PC Wurld (*totally confused*) Wally? Who's Wal ... Just a minute! Just a minute! Let's start again!

Cindy There's no time. You've *got* to arrest him before he can find Bo-Peep!

PC Wurld I know how to do my dooty, thank you. (*Going to Mefisto*) Now then. What have you got to say for yourself?

Mefisto (*laughing in his face*) Ha! Ha! Ha! (*Moving away to* L) You fools! You are too late! I have already made Bo-Peep disappear! And very soon you will join her! (*He raises his arms*)

              I summon the powers of sorcery!
              Come to my aid and work for me!

There is a crash of thunder. The lighting becomes dark and sinister

              I command you, dark forces that inhabit the night,
              Remove these meddlers from my sight!

There is a flash, followed by a complete Black-out

Freddie, Cindy and PC Wurld exit

Mefisto's laughter is heard. When the Lights return to normal, Freddie, Cindy and PC Wurld have disappeared

Mefisto Ha! Ha! Oh, I'm working well today! The Place of the Disappeared must be getting pretty crowded by now.

Lady Sneering enters from DL, *looking very annoyed*

Lady S I can't find Freddie anywhere!

Mefisto You won't. He's gone. (*Very pleased with himself*) I have just made him disappear!

Lady S (*exploding*) You did *what?!* (*Hitting him with her bag*) *You blundering blockhead! You clumsy cretin!*

Mefisto (*cowering away*) Is there something wrong?

Lady S (*fuming*) *Wrong!* Oh, yes, there's something wrong! You have only made my fabulous Freddie disappear, *that's what's wrong!* Why do you think I wanted Bo-Peep out of the way? Because I was jealous of her hair extensions? No! It was because I wanted to have Freddie Fairacre all to myself! (*Hitting him again*) *You bungling buffoon! You fumbling fool!*

Mefisto I'm sorry, your ladyship. I had no idea that ——

Lady S (*snarling at him*) *Get him back at once!*

Mefisto Yes ... (*Hastily raising his arms*)
                                    I summon the powers of sorcery!
                                    Come to my aid and work for me!

There is a great clap of thunder. The lighting becomes dark and sinister

                                    I command you, dark forces that inhabit the night,
                                    Return fabulous Freddie once more to our sight!

He makes a magic pass. Nothing happens!

Lady S What's wrong? Where is he?

Mefisto (*flustered*) I don't know! ... It doesn't seem to be working!

Lady S Try again!

Mefisto   I command you, dark forces that inhabit the night,
                                    Return fabulous Freddie once more to our sight!

Again he makes a magic pass. Again nothing!

I've overtaxed my powers! (*Pitifully*) It's put strain on my astral plane!

Lady S (*seething with rage and approaching him with raised handbag*) *Yoooou!!*

Mefisto Wait! There may be a way to get him back. But it would mean having to go to — *The Place of the Disappeared!*

Lady S Then what are you waiting for? Go there at once and bring Freddie back!

Mefisto (*nervously*) But ... I've never been there before ...

Lady S Well, now's your chance! And *I* will go with you! To make sure you don't mess things up again. *Get on with it!*

Mefisto (*raising his arms*) I command you, dark forces ...

Lady S (*threateningly*) There had better be no error!

Mefisto (*carrying on*) Transport us both to that limbo of terror!
                                    Take us to that world, so strange and weird!
                                    Take us to — *The Place of the Disappeared!*

There is a flash, followed by a Black-out. Sinister music to cover the scene change

Scene 5

The Place of the Disappeared

It is a place of nightmares. Everything is distorted and surreal. It is not a nice place to find yourself in! (See Production Notes) The lighting is weird and eerie, and is constantly changing. Ground mist swirls, and unearthly sounds fill the air. Entrances at the back and R and L

The Chorus and Dancers, as Dwellers of the Place, emerge from various directions. They wear ragged hooded cloaks, giving them a ghoulish and menacing appearance. They go into their strange and sinister dance

Song 16

After the dance, the Dwellers exit at the back

Fanny creeps on from R, followed by Bo-Peep and the Duo. They nervously take in their sinister surroundings

Fanny Ooh! This is creepy! I don't think we're in Kansas anymore! (*Spotting the audience*) Oh! Hello, folks! Well, that murky magician did it! He went and disappeared us! (*To the others*) Where d'you think we are? What is this place?

Dong Well, it's not the [local pub/club]! Unless they've had a makeover!

Bo-Peep This is where I came when Mefisto made me disappear in the show tent. I was only here for a few minutes, but I recognize it. This must be (*she looks about in awe*) The Place of the Disappeared!

Fanny Very nice, very cosy, very Gardeners' World — I *don't* think! Let's find a bus and get out of here!

Bo-Peep I don't think that's possible. Unless Mefisto makes us reappear, I think we're stuck here for good.

Fanny Y'mean — *forever?*

Bo-Peep I'm afraid it looks that way.

Fanny Oh, no! That means I'll never find out what happens to [character in TV Soap]!

From off stage, on both sides, the sheep are heard bleating

Bo-Peep Shh! What's that? *Listen!*

Fanny It sounds like ... Yes, it is! *It's sheep!*

Bo-Peep *My* sheep! I'd recognize them anywhere! Oh, the poor things! We must find them at once!

Fanny (*looking right and left*) But which way?
Ding You two look *that* way! (*Indicating* R) We'll look *this* way!
Fanny Right! (*To the audience*) And if *you* see the sheep, you'll give us a shout, won't yah?
Audience Yes!
Fanny Shout *"Sheep"* as loud as you can!

Fanny and Bo-Peep rush out R. *The Duo rush out* L

The bleating fades out. A slight pause

Wally wanders on at the back, nervously taking in his surroundings. He drifts downstage, and reacts at seeing the audience

Wally Ahh! Oh, 'tis only you, folks. Ugh! Oi don't like this place! It reminds oi of [topical/local reference to suit]!

The Dwellers creep on at the back. They advance towards Wally. The audience will be shouting warnings

(*Nervously*) W ... what is it? Is there something there?
Audience Yes!
Wally Where?
Audience Behind you!

Comic business as Wally turns around with the Dwellers keeping behind him. This business is repeated as desired. Eventually, Wally comes face to face with the Dwellers

Wally yells with fright, and runs out at the back, with the Dwellers in pursuit

Bleating, the Sheep enter from R. *The audience shout "Sheep". The Sheep exit* L. *Fanny and Bo-Peep rush on from* R

Bo-Peep (*to the audience*) Which way did they go?
Audience That way!
Fanny (*pointing* L) This way?
Audience Yes!
Fanny ⎫ (*together*) Thanks!
Bo-Peep ⎭

Bo-Peep and Fanny run out L

Wally runs on yelling at the back. The Dwellers are still pursuing him.
They chase him around the stage, and out again at the back

The Sheep enter from L

The audience shout

The Sheep exit R. *The Duo rush on from* L

Duo Which way did they go?
Audience That way!
Duo (*pointing* R) *This* way?
Audience Yes!
Duo Thanks!

Ding and Dong rush out R. *Mefisto and Lady Sneering enter at the back.*
They are about to advance downstage, when the Sheep run on from R

The audience shouts. Mefisto and Lady Sneering retreat to the back

The Sheep run out L. *Bo-Peep and Fanny run on from* R

Bo-Peep (*to the audience*) Which way did they go?
Audience That way!
Fanny (*pointing* L) This way?
Audience Yes!
Bo-Peep ⎫
Fanny ⎭ (*together*) Thanks!

Bo-Peep and Fanny run out L

Mefisto and Lady Sneering are about to move down

Ding and Dong run on from R

Mefisto and Lady Sneering retreat again

Ding ⎫
Dong ⎭ (*together, to the audience*) Which way did they go?
Audience That way!
Ding ⎫
Dong ⎭ (*together, pointing to* L) This way?
Audience Yes!

Ding } (*together*) Thanks!
Dong }

They run out L

Mefisto and Lady Sneering are about to move down

Wally runs on from R, *yelling. The Dwellers still pursue him*

Mefisto and Lady Sneering retreat again

The Dwellers chase Wally out L

Mefisto and Lady Sneering look both ways, decide it is safe, and come downstage

Mefisto They all seem to be here, don't they?
Lady S (*sneering at the audience*) Including *these* miserable minions!
Mefisto Yes! I can't understand how *they* got here!
Lady S But I don't see Freddie! Where is he?
Mefisto (*shrugging*) How would I know? When I send people to this place I don't know what happens to them. As I told you, I've never been here before. (*Looking about, admiringly*) It's rather picturesque, don't you think?
Lady S Never mind that! This is not *Location, Location, Location!* (*Snarling at him*) Find me Freddie!
Mefisto Yes, your ladyship ... Perhaps one of the others knows where he is ...

Wally runs on from L. *He bends over to get his breath back*

Lady S *There's one!*
Wally (*seeing them and yelling*) Ahhhgh!

Wally runs out L

Lady S After him! Don't let him get away!

They run out after Wally. The sheep run on from R

The audience shouts

The sheep exit L. *Bo-Peep runs on from* R

Bo-Peep (*to the audience*) Which way did they go?
Audience That way!
Bo-Peep (*pointing* L) This way?
Audience Yes!
Bo-Peep Thanks!

Bo-Peep runs out L

Ding and Dong creep on backwards from R. *Fanny creeps on backwards from* L. *Comic business as they circle each other. Eventually, their posteriors touch, and they all let out a yell*

Fanny Oooh! You made me jump! My whole life flashed before me! All twenty-five years of it! (*Looking about*) Where's Bo-Peep?
Ding ⎫ (*together*) We dunno!
Dong ⎭
Fanny (*to the audience*) Have you seen her, folks?
Audience Yes!
Ding ⎫ (*together*) Which way did she go?
Dong ⎭
Audience That way!
All (*pointing* L) *This* way?!
Audience Yes!
All Thanks!

They run out L

Wally runs on from R, *being pursued by Mefisto and Lady Sneering. They chase him out* L

Freddie, Cindy and PC Wurld enter at the back. They gaze around at their sinister surroundings

Cindy Ugh! What an awful place!
Freddie Yes. Bo-Peep was right. She said it was like being in a nightmare.
PC Wurld Would someone mind telling me what's goin' on? Where are we? How did we get here?
Freddie When Mefisto made us disappear this is where we ended up. In the Place of the Disappeared.
PC Wurld (*flustered*) But ... but that's against the law! He can't do that!
Freddie I'm afraid he has!
PC Wurld (*fumbling for his notebook*) I shall have to investigate this!

Fanny (*off* L, *calling*) *Bo-Peep? Where are you?*
Freddie That sounds like ...

Fanny enters from R, *followed by Ding and Dong*

Freddie Mum!
Fanny Freddie! Oh, thank goodness for that! A rescue party!
Freddie I'm afraid we're not, Mum. Mefisto made *us* disappear too. We're all in the same boat. Where's Bo-Peep?
Fanny She's here somewhere looking for the lost sheep.
Cindy And Wally?
Fanny (*astounded*) Don't tell me *he's* here as well! Crikey! Who's lookin' after the farm? Oh! What a mess!
PC Wurld I'll take charge here!
Fanny Oh, great! And what are you gonna do? Call for back-up?
PC Wurld We must locate the missing persons and find a way out of here.
Fanny (*sarcastically*) That's brilliant, Poirot! We'd never have thought of that!
Freddie (*to PC Wurld*) What do you suggest?
PC Wurld We will split up and make a search. (*To Cindy, Ding and Dong*) You three look *that* way! (*He points* L. *To Freddie and Fanny*) We'll look *that* way! (*He points to* R) Right! Go, *go, go!*

They exit R *and* L

Wally enters at the back and staggers downstage

Wally (*to the audience, gasping*) Oi ... oi think oi've given them two nasties the slip! (*He bends over to get his breath back*)

Mefisto enters from R. *At the same time, Lady Sneering enters from* L. *They creep towards the unsuspecting Wally*

The audience will be shouting warnings, but he takes no notice. As he straightens up, they both grab hold of him

Wally (*Wailing*) Oh, no! 'Ere we go again! Who are you lookin' for *this* time?
Lady S } (*together*) Freddie!
Mefisto }
Wally Wull, oi bain't him! Can't you tell by the legs!
Lady S Where is he? *Tell us!* (*She twists his arm*)

Wally *Aooow!*

The Dwellers enter from R *and* L. *Unseen, they move to each side of the others*

Mefisto If you don't tell us where he is it will be the worse for you!
Lady S Tell us! Where is he? *Where is Freddie? (She twists his arm)*
Wally *Aooow!* Oi don't know! *Oi don't know! (He catches sight of the Dwellers)* Why don't you ask them?
Mefisto ⎫
Lady S ⎬ *(together)* Who?
Wally *Them!*

Mefisto and Lady Sneering turn and see the Dwellers

Mefisto ⎫
Lady S ⎬ *(together; yelling with fright)* Ahhhhhgh!!
Wally ⎭

Mefisto, Lady Sneering and Wally run out at the back still yelling, pursued by the Dwellers

Fanny, Freddie and PC Wurld enter from R. *At the same time, Cindy and the Duo enter from* L. *They are all calling "Bo-Peep? Wally? Where are you?" They meet in the middle*

Fanny ⎫
Freddie ⎬ *(together, to the others)* Any luck?
PC Wurld ⎭
Cindy ⎫
Ding ⎬ *(together)* No!
Dong ⎭
PC Wurld Keep looking!

They resume calling for the others

Fanny, Freddie and PC Wurld exit L. *Cindy and the Duo exit* R

Bo-Peep enters at the back and comes forward

Bo-Peep *(to the audience)* Oh, dear! I can't find the sheep anywhere! Have *you* seen them?
Audience No!

Bo-Peep And I don't know what's happened to Mrs Fairacre and the others. This place is so scary. I can't bear the thought of staying here ... all alone ... without ever seeing Freddie again. (*She buries her face in her hands and weeps*)

The Dwellers creep on from R and L. They advance on the unsuspecting Bo-Peep

The audience will be shouting warnings, but the poor girl is too upset to notice. The Dwellers are just about to reach out for her

Freddie enters from L

Freddie Bo!
Bo-Peep (*looking up*) Freddie? (*She then sees the Dwellers and screams*)
Freddie (*rushing at the Dwellers and yelling*) Get away from her! Leave her alone!

Obviously frightened, the Dwellers run out in all directions

Freddie and Bo-Peep rush into each other's arms

Freddie You're safe now.
Bo-Peep Oh, Freddie! I thought I'd never see you again. How did you get here? Did Mefisto make you disappear too?
Freddie (*trying to make light of it*) No, I came by [local taxi firm]. Yes, he did.
Bo-Peep How are we going to get away from this awful place? What are we going to do, Freddie?
Freddie I wish I knew. At least we're together.

Freddie and Bo-Peep cuddle

Fanny and PC Wurld enter from L. At the same time, Cindy and the Duo enter from R

Fanny He's at it again!
Freddie (*still cuddling Bo-Peep*) I've found her, Mum.
Fanny I can see that! (*To the audience*) Tch! These youngsters! Any excuse for a canoodle!
Cindy What about Wally?
Fanny (*to Freddie, indicating the cuddle*) You haven't got *him* in there as well, have yah?

Wally staggers on from R

Cindy Wally!
Wally Cindy!

They rush into each other's arms and embrace

Fanny (*amazed*) Well, I'll be ... (*To the audience*) Looks like he scored
   after all, folks! There's hope for me yet!
PC Wurld Is that all the missing persons accounted for?
Bo-Peep All except the sheep! We've still got to find *them!*

Suddenly, Lady Sneering enters from L

The others react

Lady S Hello, Freddie.
Freddie Lady Sneering! What are you doing here?
Lady S I've come to take you home with me.
Freddie Can you get us away from here?
Lady S No, but I know a man who can!

Mefisto enters from L. *The others react*

PC Wurld (*to Mefisto*) Ah! You've seen the error of your ways, eh.
   Come to get us out of here, have you?
Mefisto }
Lady S } (*together*) Ha! Ha! Ha!
Fanny (*to PC Wurld*) I think you've got that wrong, Columbo!
Lady S The only ones to leave this place will be myself, Mefisto and
   Freddie! You, Little Bo-Peep — *will not!* (*With a snarl, she drags
   Bo-Peep from Freddie and pushes her away*) You and the rest of these
   miserable morons will remain here — *forever!*

*The others react, horrified. Mefisto and Lady Sneering indulge in more
evil laughter*

Freddie (*to Lady Sneering*) But ... why are you doing this? *Why?*
Lady S (*taking his arm, seductively*) My dear boy. As soon as we get
   back, I will show you why ... *and how!*
Freddie But I don't understand ...
Fanny *I* do! Don't yah see? That's what all this disappearin' lark's been
   about! That's why she wanted Bo-Peep out of the way! *She fancies
   you, Freddie!* (*To Lady Sneering*) Don't yah?

Lady S To put it crudely — yes!
Fanny Disgustin'! You're old enough to be his mother! You're old enough to be *my* mother!
Freddie But I love Bo-Peep! I haven't any feelings for you!
Lady S Oh, *I* will do all the feeling! (*To Mefisto*) Let us waste no more time! Send the three of us back at once!
Mefisto   I summon the powers of sorcery! Come to my aid and work for me!

There is a great crash of thunder. The lighting becomes even more strange and sinister. General panic!

Fanny (*yelling in desperation*) Somebody do something!
Mefisto Ha! Ha! Ha! You can do nothing! You are all powerless! None of you can defeat the mighty Mefisto!

Suddenly, Merdalf, wearing a hood to disguise himself, enters from L. *The Dwellers appear at the back and sides*

Merdalf That's true! But *I* can! (*He throws back his hood*)
Mefisto (*recoiling*) You!
Merdalf Yes! It is *I*! Merdalf, the magnificent!
Lady S (*to Mefisto*) Who is this person?
Merdalf Allow me to explain. Many years ago, Mefisto and I were fellow students at the college for advanced sorcery. My knowledge and skills were always far superior to his. And I was always the popular one. Overwhelmed with jealously, he contrived to make me disappear, and I found myself in this dreadful place. I have languished in this loathsome limbo ever since, along with these other poor wretches. (*Indicating the Dwellers*) All victims of his foul misuse of magic. Until now I have been powerless! But meeting him again, face to face, will enable me to take my revenge!
Mefisto *No!* (*He tries to make an escape*)

Two of the Dwellers seize Mefisto

Fanny What are you gonna do to him? We've got a few suggestions! (*To the audience*) Haven't we, folks?

The audience give their suggestions!

Merdalf (*to the audience*) All very suitable, I'm sure. But I think I know the most befitting punishment! (*He raises his arms*)

> I summon the powers of sorcery!
> Come to my aid and work for me!

There is a great crash of thunder. The lighting changes once again. All react. Mefisto cowers in fear

> You will have cause to rue this day,
> For I mean to take your powers away!
> And as you are hated by everyone here,
> I will also make you — *disappear!* (*He makes a magic pass at Mefisto*)

There is a flash, followed by a complete Black-out. Loud, dramatic music. Strange, unearthly sounds fill the air

Mefisto and the Dwellers exit

The Lights come up. We are back on the sunlit village green! [See Production Notes]. All look about in wonderment and joy

Fanny We're back home again!
All Hurray!
Freddie (*to Merdalf*) How did that happen?
Merdalf When I made Mefisto disappear his spell over you disappeared with him.
Fanny (*to the audience*) That's neat, isn't it? You can't say you don't get value for money.

Lady Sneering sneaks towards an exit

> (*Seeing this, bellowing*) *Oy!* Not so fast, Lady Muck! You were in cahoots with that mouldy magician! (*To Merdalf*) How about doin' something really nasty to *her!* (*To the audience*) Got any ideas, folks?

They will probably have several!

PC Wurld That won't be necessary. (*Planting his hand firmly on Lady Sneering's shoulder*) I arrest you in the name of the law!
Lady S (*outraged*) *What!* You can't do that! I am one of the landed gentry!
PC Wurld You're *landed* all right! You'll be charged with conspiracy, kidnappin' and interferin' with a police officer in the course of his dooty! You're goin' down, m'lady!

All (*cheering*) Hurray!

Fanny That'll teach yah! Tryin' to nick someone else's boyfriend!

PC Wurld You come along with me!

PC Wurld leads the protesting Lady Sneering out. She still manages to sneer at the others and the audience as she goes

Everyone is happy, with the exception of Cindy, who is looking downcast. Wally becomes aware of this

Wally (*to Cindy*) Cheer up, Cindy. What's wrong? (*Proudly*) You've got *me* now.

Fanny Yes! Everything a woman could want! (*To the audience*) If she doesn't want much!

Cindy (*sadly*) I was just thinking. With Mefisto gone we've lost our main attraction. The show will have to close down.

Ding
Dong } (*equally sad*) That's true.

Merdalf If you are you looking for a replacement, I would be more than happy to offer *my* services.

Cindy (*brightening*) You would?

Merdalf Yes. It's not easy trying to find work as a magician, y'know. It creates such confusion at the Job Centre.

Cindy Then consider yourself engaged. When can you start?

Merdalf As soon as you like. But first I must return to my home. I haven't been back there for a very long time.

Freddie Where is your home?

Merdalf [name of a nearby town or village]! (*He moves to an exit, and turns*) Au revoir!

There is a flash and Merdalf has gone

Fanny Fancy him livin' in [town/village mentioned]! Still, they could do with a miracle worker there! Well, that's worked out very well, hasn't it?

The others all agree

Bo-Peep (*with sudden alarm*) Oh, no!

Fanny What's up now?

Bo-Peep *The sheep!* We forgot all about the sheep! Did they come back with us, or ——

This is soon answered

Bleating loudly, the Sheep enter

Everyone cheers, and makes a great fuss of them

The Villagers/Farmhands and the Show Dancers enter. Even Buttercup can put in an appearance, if desired

Bo-Peep   (*to the audience*) Now that's what I call a really happy ending.
Fanny   (*to the audience*) Well, a *really* happy ending would be me winnin' the lottery and datin' [current heart-throb]! But I suppose we'll have to settle for this. (*To the Conductor/Pianist*) *Take it away!*

Song 17

A joyful song and dance involving everyone. The number ends with a tableau, and the Lights fade to Black-out

The Tabs close, or the front cloth is lowered

SCENE 6

Near the farm

Tabs, or as Act I, Scene 2

Wally enters from DR. *He is singing at the top of his voice and making a terrible, off key noise! Fanny enters from* DL

Fanny   (*to the audience*) What's goin' on?! Who's being cruel to that pussy cat?! (*Reacting to Wally*) Oh, it's wailin' Wally! (*Going to him*) *Oy!* That's enough of that! Put a sock in it! (*Yelling*) *Shuuurup!!* (*Wally stops*) What d'you think you're doing?
Wally   Singin'!
Fanny   Singing! Are you sure? It sounded like you were havin' trouble with your zip again!
Wally   Oi be practising.
Fanny   What for? Are you gonna get a job as a burglar alarm?
Wally   Oi be givin' up farmin' an' joinin' Cindy's show. (*Proudly*) Oi'm gonna be a singist!
Fanny   Does Cindy know about this?
Wally   Ar! She said oi've got the X factor!

Fanny You haven't even got *Max Factor!*
Wally She said there's a big opening for someone like oi.
Fanny Yes. It's called a manhole! Well, you'll never get anywhere with a
voice like yours. It's awful! It's terrible! (*To the audience*) Isn't it, folks?
Audience Yes!
Wally (*to them*) Oh, no, it isn't!
Audience Oh, yes, it is!
Wally Oh, no, it isn't!
Audience Oh, yes, it is!
Wally (*to Fanny*) Oi bet they can't sing as good as wot oi does.
Fanny *Wot oi does!* That's shocking! Where's your grammar?
Wally At 'ome with me Granfer! (*He guffaws*) Anyhow, oi bet they can't.
Fanny I bet they can! In fact, we're gonna give 'em the chance to prove
it. (*To the audience*) Oh, yes! You thought you'd got away with it,
didn't you? And don't think you can make a run for it. We've locked
all the doors! (*To Wally*) Have you got the words?
Wally Not since oi went to the vet.
Fanny I said *words*, not *worms!*
Wally Oh, ar! (*He signals to off stage*)

Ding enters DR *and Dong enters* DL. *Both carry large song sheets with
words for a different song on each*

Fanny Oh, here they are! Ant and Dec! (*Or other duo*)
Dong Where do you want us to stand?
Fanny Somewhere in the Himalayas would be nice! No, stay where you
are. (*To the audience*) Now, this is what we want you to do. We want
this side to sing *that* song. (*She points to Ding's sheet*) And *this* side to
sing *that* song. (*She points to Dong's sheet*) Let's give a try. *This* side
first! (*To the Conductor/Pianist*) Hand brake off, dear!

Song 18

*They have fun getting one side of the audience to sing, and then the other
side. They have even more fun getting both sides sing their songs at the
same time! If Fanny needs time to change into a special finale costume,
she can leave the other three to it. If desired, the house lights can be
brought up, and children from the audience can be invited on to the
stage and asked their names and ages, etc.*

The children return to their seats and the house lights go down

Waving goodbye to the audience, those on stage run out

The Lights fade to black-out. A fanfare sounds

Scene 7

The Grand Finale

A special Finale setting, or the Village Green can be used with added decorations. Bright lighting and bouncy music. The full company enter for the walk down and take their bows. The last to enter are Freddie and Bo-Peep, magnificently attired

Freddie	The time has come for us to go.
Bo-Peep	We hope you have enjoyed the show.
Ding	We've done our best to make you happy.
Dong	Even though the jokes were...

All look at him

	... snappy?
Wally	Cindy's the girl that oi adore!
Fanny	With her I thought he'd *never* score.
Cindy	All other boys my Wally surpasses.
Fanny	Per'aps she needs to get some glasses!
Lady S	You common trash! You're base and low!
PC Wurld	They're fixing her with a nice ASBO!
Mefisto	I shall return! My day will come!
Merdalf	Accept defeat. You've had it, chum.
Fanny	The sheep would like to say *ta-ta*.
	Here's their final
Sheep	*Baa! Baa! Baa!*
Bo-Peep	So with that message from my sheep,
	It's a fond farewell from —
All	(*waving*) *Little Bo-Peep!*

Song 19

Or a reprise

Curtain

FURNITURE AND PROPERTY LIST

Further dressing may be added at the director's discretion

ACT I

Scene 1

On stage: Back cloth showing countryside and Fanny's farm
Village Green side wings representing cottages, shops and trees
Inn entrance with hanging sign board

Off stage: Drum (**Ding**)
Cymbals (**Dong**)
Toilet roll (**Wally**)
Shepherd's crook (**Bo-Peep**)

Personal: **Lady Sneering**: Bag. *In it*: two large wads of bank notes
(throughout)

Scene 2

On stage: Tabs, or front cloth showing a picturesque country road

Scene 3

On stage: Back cloth and side wings representing show tent interior
Raised platform with rows of benches
2 smaller single benches

Off stage: Small table. *On it*: black cloth decorated with magic symbols;
paraphernalia needed for conjuring tricks (**Ding** and **Dong**)

Personal: **Dong**: coin
Mefisto: any concealed props necessary for conjuring tricks

Scene 4

On stage: Tabs, or front cloth as used in Act I, Scene 2

Furniture and Property List   75

SCENE 5

On stage: Village Green setting as used in Act I, Scene 1

Off stage: Tankards (**Villagers**)
               Trays (**Barmaids**)
               Shepherd's crook (**Bo-Peep**)

ACT II

SCENE 1

On stage: Back cloth showing countryside and village
               Farmyard side wings
               Fence
               Farmhouse
               Barn
               Metal bucket and ladle
               Plastic bucket and milking stool

Off stage: Prop milk bottle, packet of prop butter, box of prop
               chocolates (**Buttercup**, hidden)

SCENE 2

On stage: Tabs, or front cloth as used in Act I, Scene 2

Personal: **Wally**: enormous flower in button hole

SCENE 3

On stage: Show tent interior as used in Act I, Scene 3

Personal: **Cindy**: clown mask
               Dancers: clown masks

SCENE 4

On stage: Tabs, or front cloth used in Act I, Scene 2

Off stage: Notebook and pencil (**PC Wurld**)

Scene 5

On stage: Indefinable shapes and cyclorama or back cloth
                      showing surreal landscape
                  Strange, surreal side wings
                  Pre-set — village green setting for transformation scene

Scene 6

On stage: Tabs, or front cloth used in Act I, Scene 2

Off stage: Song sheets (**Ding** and **Dong**)

Scene 7

On stage: Special Finale setting, or Village Green with added decorations

LIGHTING PLOT

Property fittings: nil
Various interior and exterior settings

ACT I, SCENE 1

To open: General exterior lighting

Cue 1	Song 3 *Romantic lighting with follow spot on* **Freddie**	(Page 4)
Cue 2	End of Song 3 *Take out spot and romantic lighting. Return to previous setting*	(Page 4)
Cue 3	**Mefisto**: "Come to my aid and work for me!" *Dark and sinister lighting*	(Page 11)
Cue 4	There is a flash *The lighting returns to normal*	(Page 11)
Cue 5	Song 5 *Romantic lighting with follow spots on* **Freddie** *and* **Bo Peep**	(Page 12)
Cue 6	End of Song 5 *Fade lights to black-out*	(Page 12)

ACT I, SCENE 2

To open: General exterior lighting

Cue 7	Song 6 *Follow spots on* **Cindy**, **Ding** *and* **Dong**	(Page 14)
Cue 8	End of Song 6 *Take out spots*	(Page 14)
Cue 9	**Mefisto** exits *Fade lights to black-out*	(Page 16)

ACT I, SCENE 3

To open: Interior lighting in show tent

Cue 10	Song 7 *Follow spots on* **Cindy** *and* **Dancers**	(Page 18)
Cue 11	End of Song 7 *Take out follow spots*	(Page 18)
Cue 12	Alternative "act" (optional) *Follow spot*	(Page 19)
Cue 13	End of alternative "act" (optional) *Take out follow spot*	(Page 19)
Cue 14	**Mefisto** goes into his conjuring act *Spot on* **Mefisto**	(Page 21)
Cue 15	Applause from spectators *Take out spot*	(Page 21)
Cue 16	**Mefisto**: "Come to my aid and work for me!" *Dark and sinister lighting*	(Page 21)
Cue 17	**Mefisto**: "... and disappear from sight!" Then a flash *Complete black-out. Allow time for* **Bo-Peep** *to exit,* *then Lights return to normal*	(Page 21)
Cue 18	**Mefisto**: "... and return to our sight!" Then a flash *Complete black-out. Allow time for* **Bo-Peep** *to enter,* *then Lights return to normal*	(Page 22)
Cue 19	**Lady Sneering** exits *Fade to black-out*	(Page 24)

ACT I, SCENE 4

To open: General exterior lighting

Cue 20	Reprise of Song 5 (optional) *Romantic lighting and follow spots* *on* **Freddie** *and* **Bo-Peep**	(Page 25)

| *Cue* 21 | End of reprise (optional)
Take out spots and romantic lighting.
Return to previous setting | (Page 25) |

| *Cue* 22 | **Lady Sneering** exits
Fade to black-out | (Page 27) |

ACT I, SCENE 5

To open: General exterior lighting

| *Cue* 23 | Song 9
Follow spots on **Bo-Peep** *and* **Sheep** | (Page 30) |

| *Cue* 24 | End of Song 9
Take out spots | (Page 30) |

| *Cue* 25 | **Mefisto**: "Come to my aid and work for me!"
Dark and sinister lighting | (Page 30) |

| *Cue* 26 | **Mefisto** makes a magic pass at the sheep,
then a flash
Black-out. Allow time for sheep to exit,
then Lights return to normal | (Page 31) |

ACT II, SCENE 1

To open: General exterior lighting

| *Cue* 27 | **Mefisto**: "Come to my aid and work for me!"
Dark and sinister lighting | (Page 42) |

| *Cue* 28 | **Buttercup** trots on
Lights return quickly to normal | (Page 42) |

| *Cue* 29 | End of Song 11
Fade lights to black-out | (Page 43) |

ACT II, SCENE 2

To open: General exterior lighting

| *Cue* 30 | Song 12
Follow spot on **Ding** *and* **Dong** | (Page 44) |

| *Cue* 31 | End of Song 12
Take out follow spot | (Page 44) |

Cue 32   **Ding** and **Dong** exit   (Page 47)
              Fade lights to black-out

ACT II, Scene 3

To open: General tent interior lighting

Cue 33   Song 13   (Page 47)
              Follow spots on **Cindy** *and* **Dancers**

Cue 34   End of Song 13   (Page 47)
              Take out spots

Cue 35   Song 14   (Page 49)
              Follow spots on **Wally** *and* **Cindy**

Cue 36   End of Song 14   (Page 49)
              Take out follow spots

Cue 37   **Mefisto**: "Come to my aid and work for me!"   (Page 52)
              Dark and sinister lighting

Cue 38   **Mefisto**: " ... and take him from our sight!"   (Page 52)
                  Then a flash
              Complete black-out. Allow time for **Wally** *to exit,*
                  then Lights return to normal

Cue 39   **Cindy** exits   (Page 52)
              Fade lights to black-out

ACT II, Scene 4

To open: General exterior lighting

Cue 40   Song 15   (Page 53)
              Romantic lighting and follow spots
                  on **Freddie** *and* **Bo-Peep**

Cue 41   End of Song 15   (Page 53)
              Take out romantic lighting and follow spots.
                  Return to previous setting

Cue 42   **Mefisto**: "Come to my aid and work for me!"   (Page 56)
              Dark and sinister lighting

Cue 43	**Mefisto**: " ... these four persons from our sight!"	(Page 56)
	Then a flash	
	Complete black-out. Allow time for **Fanny**,	
	Bo-Peep, **Ding** *and* **Dong** *to exit, then Lights*	
	return to normal	
Cue 44	**Mefisto**: "Come to my aid and work for me!"	(Page 57)
	Dark and sinister lighting	
Cue 45	**Mefisto**: "Remove these meddlers from my sight!"	(Page 57)
	Then a flash	
	Complete black-out. Allow time for Freddie,	
	Cindy and PC Wurld to exit, then Lights	
	return to normal	
Cue 46	**Mefisto**: "Come to my aid and work for me!"	(Page 58)
	Dark and sinister lighting	
Cue 47	**Mefisto**: "... *The Place of the Disappeared!*"	
	Then a flash	(Page 58)
	Black-out	

ACT II, SCENE 5

To open: Strange and eerie lighting, constantly changing
throughout the scene

Cue 48	**Mefisto**: "Come to my aid and work for me!"	(Page 68)
	Lighting becomes even more strange and sinister	
Cue 49	**Merdalf**: "Come to my aid and work for me!"	(Page 69)
	Lighting changes again	
Cue 50	**Merdalf**: "I will also make you — *disappear!*"	(Page 69)
	Then a flash	
	Complete black-out. Allow time for **Mefisto** *and*	
	Dwellers *to exit, and for transformation to*	
	Village Green. Return to bright general	
	exterior lighting	
Cue 51	End of Song 17	(Page 71)
	Fade to black-out	

ACT II, SCENE 6

To open: General exterior lighting

Cue 52   Song 18   (Page 72)
               Bring up house lights

Cue 53   End of Song 18   (Page 72)
               Take out house lights

Cue 54   **Fanny**, **Wally**, **Ding** and **Dong** exit   (Page 72)
               Fade lights to black-out

ACT II, SCENE 7

To open: Bright general lighting with follow spots on cast as they
               enter and take their bows

No cues

USE OF COPYRIGHT MUSIC

A licence issued by Samuel French Ltd to perform this play does not include permission to use the Incidental music specified in this copy. Where the place of performance is already licensed by the PERFORMING RIGHT SOCIETY a return of the music used must be made to them. If the place of performance is not so licensed then application should be made to the Performing Right Society, 29 Berners Street, London W1T 3AB (website: www.mcps-prs-alliance.co.uk).

A separate and additional licence from PHONOGRAPHIC PERFORMANCE LTD, 1 Upper James Street, London W1F 9DE (website: www.ppluk.com) is needed whenever commercial recordings are used.

EFFECTS PLOT

ACT I

Cue 1   **Fanny**: "... or whatever his name is?"   (Page 10)
Flash

Cue 2   **Mefisto**: "Come to my aid and work for me!"   (Page 11)
Great crash of thunder

Cue 3   **Mefisto**: " ... for all to see!"   (Page 11)
Flash

Cue 4   The music comes to an end. A hush falls   (Page 17)
A fanfare sounds

Cue 5   **Voice**: "Prepare to meet — the mighty Mefisto!"   (Page 20)
Flash

Cue 6   **Mefisto**: "Come to my aid and work for me!"   (Page 21)
Great crash of thunder

Cue 7   **Mefisto**: "... and disappear from sight!"   (Page 21)
Flash

Cue 8   **Mefisto**: "... and return to our sight!"   (Page 22)
Flash

Cue 9   **Mefisto**: "Come to my aid and work for me!"   (Page 30)
Great crash of thunder

Cue 10   **Mefisto** makes a magic pass at the sheep   (Page 31)
Flash

ACT II

Cue 11   **Mefisto**: "Come to my aid and work for me!"   (Page 42)
Great crash of thunder

Cue 12   **Mefisto**: "Come to my aid and work for me!"   (Page 52)
Great crash of thunder

Cue 13	**Mefisto**: " ... and take him from our sight!" *Flash*	(Page 52)
Cue 14	**Mefisto**: "Come to my aid and work for me!" *Crash of thunder*	(Page 56)
Cue 15	**Mefisto**: "Remove these four persons from our sight!" *Flash*	(Page 56)
Cue 16	**Mefisto**: "Come to my aid and work for me!" *Crash of thunder*	(Page 57)
Cue 17	**Mefisto**: "Remove these meddlers from my sight!" *Flash*	(Page 57)
Cue 18	**Mefisto**: "Come to my aid and work for me!" *Great clap of thunder*	(Page 58)
Cue 19	**Mefisto**: "*— The Place of the Disappeared!*" *Flash*	(Page 58)
Cue 20	To open ACT II, SCENE 5 *Ground mist. Weird background noises throughout scene until transformation*	(Page 59)
Cue 21	**Mefisto**: "Come to my aid and work for me!" *Great crash of thunder*	(Page 68)
Cue 22	**Merdalf**: "Come to my aid and work for me!" *Great crash of thunder*	(Page 69)
Cue 23	**Merdalf**: "I will also make you — disappear!" *Flash, followed by a black-out. Loud, dramatic music. Strange, unearthly sounds fill the air*	(Page 69)
Cue 24	**Merdalf**: "*Au revoir!*" *Flash*	(Page 70)
Cue 25	End of Scene 6 (lights fade to black-out) *Fanfare sounds*	(Page 73)

Lightning Source UK Ltd.
Milton Keynes UK
UKHW021305131222
413858UK00033B/401